MW01490250

BY JO PETTY

My Lamp and My Light
Words of Silver and Gold
Gifts for the Graduate
Life Is for Living

Jo Petty

FLEMING H. REVELL COMPANY

Old Tappan, New Jersey

Scripture quotations are based on
the King James Version of the Bible.

Library of Congress Cataloging in Publication Data

Petty, Jo.
Life is for living.

1. Christian life—Quotations, maxims, etc.
I. Title.
BV4501.2.P433 248'.4 78-10803
ISBN 0-8007-0978-0

Published by Fleming H. Revell Company

Printed in the United States of America

That which the fountain sends forth
returns again to the fountain.

Henry Wadsworth Longfellow

Contents

Preface

If this proves to be a good book, it will be because of the mighty theme:

> . . . the fruit of the Spirit is love, joy, peace, longsuffering, gentleness, goodness, faith, Meekness, temperance: against such there is no law.
>
> Galatians 5:22, 23

Also, it is the good reader that makes the good book. Every moment finds new ways of saying the old truths in the hope that everyone will hear. Quotations from the great old authors are an act of reverence on the part of the one who quotes and a blessing to the public.

I go to books, and especially to *The Book,* as a bee goes to the flowers, for a nectar that I can make into my own honey. I more appreciate what others comprehend than what I comprehend myself. I light my candle from their torches. I do not invent, for I find everything has already been better said than I can say it.

A well-chosen anthology is a complete dispensary of medicine for the more common mental disorders, and may be used as much for prevention as for cure. Let us, with hearts devout, declare what we have seen; and to our children's children tell how good our Lord has been!

A proverb is no proverb to you until your life has illustrated it. Here is knowledge available just for the taking—sayings of great men and women and sayings of the Greatest of the Great.

Here are thoughts that breathe and words that burn—not for an age, but for all time. Not a verse, not a single line is mine. How much better is the text since I borrowed the whole.

I can tell you no more
If I preach a whole year.

JO PETTY

The great business of life is:
To be,
To do,
To do without,
and
To depart.

Love

Love is swift, sincere, pious, pleasant, gentle, strong, patient, faithful, prudent, longsuffering, manly and never seeks her own; for when a man seeks his own, there he falls from love.

[Charity] seeketh not her own . . . .
1 Corinthians 13:5

In Faith and Hope the world will disagree,
But all mankind is concerned with Charity.

How shall we render Charity toward others when we are uncharitable to ourselves?

I gave a little tea party
This afternoon at three.
  'Twas very small,
Three guests in all—
I, myself, and me.

Myself ate up the sandwiches
While I drank all the tea,
  'Twas also I
  Who ate the pie
And passed the cake to me.

If all the world seems cold to you,
Kindle fires to warm it!

If the world's a wilderness,
Go, build houses in it!

A man does not plant a tree for himself. He plants it for posterity.

Oxen bear the yoke for others.
Bees store up honey for others.
Sheep put on their fleece for others.
What do I for others?

We shall do so much in the years to come,
But what have we done today?
We shall give our gold in a princely sum,
But what did we give today?

Can I see another's woe,
And not be in sorrow too?
Can I see another's grief,
And not seek for kind relief?

No radiant pearl which crested Fortune wears,
No gem that twinkling hangs from Beauty's ears,
Not the bright stars which Night's blue arch adorn,
Nor rising suns that gild the vernal morn,
Shine with such luster as the tear that flows
Down Virtue's manly cheek for others' woes.

Love comforts like sunshine after rain.

To love for the sake of being loved is human, but to love for the sake of loving is angelic.

Love needs no laws.

It is not so much consequence what you say as how you say it.

When Silence speaks for Love, she has much to say.

Sweet are the words of Love,
Sweeter Love's thoughts.
Sweetest of all—
What Love says nor thinks but does.

Money can be as beautiful as roses—even red roses.

'Tis not the weight of jewel or plate,
  Or the fondle of silk and fur;
'Tis the spirit in which the gift is rich,
  As the gifts of the wise ones were;

And we are not told whose gift was gold
Or whose was the gift of myrrh.

And when they were come into the house, they saw the young child with Mary his mother, and fell down, and worshipped him: and when they had opened their treasures, they presented unto him gifts; gold, and frankincense, and myrrh.

Matthew 2:11

True love's the gift which God has given
To man alone beneath the heaven:
It is not fantasy's hot fire,
Whose wishes, soon as granted, fly;
It lives not in fierce desire,
With dead desire it does not die;
It is the secret sympathy,
The silver link, the silken tie,
Which heart to heart and mind to mind
In body and in soul can bind.

Love is indestructible,
Its holy flame burns forever.

All love is sweet,
Given or returned.
Common as light is love,
And its familiar voice wearies not ever . . . .

Talk not of wasted affection! Affection never was wasted. If it enrich not the heart of another, its waters, returning back to their springs, like the rain, shall fill them full of refreshment. That which the fountain sends forth returns again to the fountain.

Benefactors appear to love in a greater degree those whom they benefit than those who are benefitted love their benefactors.

> There is a heaven, forever, day by day,
> The upward longing of my soul does tell me so.
> There is a hell, I'm quite as sure: for pray,
> If there were not, where would my neighbors go?

I buried the hatchet, but I remember where I buried it.

Those hateful to us we are not to hate.

> . . . Love your enemies, bless them that curse you, do good to them that hate you, and pray for them which despitefully use you, and persecute you;
>
> That ye may be the children of your Father which is in heaven: for he maketh his sun to rise on the evil and on the good, and sendeth rain on the just and on the unjust.
>
> Matthew 5:44, 45

Love the offender, though you detest the offense.

Join your hands, and with your hands, your hearts.

> To all the gossip that I hear
> I'll give no faith; to what I see
> But only half, for it is clear
> All that led up is dark to me.

Learn we the larger life to live
To comprehend is to forgive.

If you find in me a fault,
Lock it in your memory vault,
And pray for me.

'Tis not enough to help the feeble up,
But to support them after.

Do you wonder that gold, which in itself is so useless a thing, should be everywhere so much esteemed that even men, for whom it was made, and by whom it has its value, should yet be thought of less value than it is?

Let us no more be true to boasted race or clan,
But our highest dream, the brotherhood of man.

Not till the sun excludes you do I exclude you.

The ornament of a house is the friends who frequent it.

One friend in a lifetime is much; two are many; three are hardly possible.

Two may talk and one may hear, but three cannot take part in a conversation of the most sincere and searching out.

A friend is a person with whom I may be sincere. Before him, I may think aloud.

Give smiles to those who love you less,
But keep your tears for me.

The lusty days of long ago,
When you were Bill and I was Joe.

Father calls me William,
Sister calls me Will,
Mother calls me Willie,
But the fellers call me Bill.

Have you a friend, as heart may wish at will?
Then use him so, to have his friendship still.

He that is your friend indeed,
Will help you in your time of need.

If you have a friend worth loving,
Love him. Yes, and let him know
That you love him, ere life's evening
Tinge his brow with sunset glow.
Why should good words ne'er be said
Of a friend till he is dead?

If you like him or you love him, tell him now.

To let friendship die away by negligence and silence is not wise. Throw not away one of the greatest comforts of this weary pilgrimage.

I met a stranger in the night
Whose lamp had ceased to shine.
I paused and let him light
His lamp from mine.
A tempest sprang up later on
And shook the world about

And when the wind was gone
My lamp was out.
But back to me the stranger came—
His lamp was glowing fine!
He held the precious flame
And lighted mine!

Give me a friendship that, like love, is warm.

Give me a love that is steady like friendship.

Where there is true friendship, there need be no ceremony.

Friend,
Come in the evening, or come in the morning,
Come when you're looked for, or come without warning.

A friend loveth at all times . . . .
Proverbs 17:17

Would you have a friend?
Would you know what friend is best?
Have God your friend,
Who passes all the rest.

A man builds a fine house; and now he has a master, and a task for life; he is to furnish it, watch it, show it, and keep it in repair for the rest of his days. What's wrong with that? Nothing. He does it for love's sweet sake.

No man ever lived that had enough
Of children's gratitude or woman's love.

"Oh, 'tis Love that makes us grateful,
Oh, 'tis Love that makes us rich!"
So sings man, and every fateful
Echo bears his amorous speech.

We flatter those we scarcely know,
We please the fleeting guest,
And deal full many a thoughtless blow
To those who love us best.

He may look just the same to you,
And he may be just as fine,
But the next-door dog is the next-door dog,
And mine—is—mine!

Who ran to help me when I fell,
And would some pretty story tell,
Or kiss the place to make it well?
My Mother and my Daddy.

Let those love now who never loved before;
Let those who always loved, now love the more.

So long as we love we serve.

Love yourself last.

Marriage

One pairing is as good as another, where all is venture.

But marriage is that relation between man and woman in which the independence is equal, the dependence mutual, and the obligation reciprocal.

The contract 'twixt Hannah, God and me,
Was not for one or twenty years,
But for eternity.

Ask nothing more of me, sweet,
All I can give you I give;
Heart of my heart, were it more
More would be laid at your feet.

The wishes of one become the binding obligation of the other.

All that belongs to one is the property of the other.

Love gives all and must have all in return.

Love does not wish to be happy in anything that separates us.

All for love and nothing for reward.

> My true-love has my heart, and I have his,
> By just exchange one for the other given.

> He is the half part of a blessed man,
> Left to be finished by such a she;
> And she a fair divided excellence,
> Whose fulness of perfection lies in him.

The deepest desire of each heart is that it may know every longing, that it may fly on the wings of the wind to gratify it.

A lover without indiscretion is no lover at all.

> She smiled, and the shadows departed;
> She shone, and the snows were rain;
> And he who was frozen hearted
> Bloomed up into love again.

He: My dear, I love you always, all ways and all weighs.

She: I would not be a Queen for all the world!

> With you conversing I forget all time,
> All seasons, and their change; all please alike.

So dearly I love him that with him all deaths I could endure, without him, live no life.

The quarrels of lovers are the renewal of love.

Never love unless you can
Bear with all the faults of man:
Men will sometimes jealous be,
Though but little cause they see;
And hang the head, as discontent,
And speak what straight they will repent.

She knows her man, and when you rant and swear,
Can draw you to her with a single hair.

Never a tear dims the eye
That time and patience will not dry;
Never a lip is curved with pain
That can't be kissed into smiles again.

A feeling of sadness and longing
That is not akin to pain,
And resembles sorrow only
As the mist resembles the rain.

To be loved, be lovable.

If to her some female errors fall,
Look on her face, and you'll forget them all.

Love is not love which alters when it alteration finds.

And ruined love, when it is built anew,
Grows fairer than at first, more strong,
far greater.

The fire which seems extinguished often slumbers beneath the ashes.

Marriage is a thing you've got to give your whole mind to.

The man who loves a woman as much as she wants to be loved has no time for outside flirtations.

My wife had few other thoughts than to love and be loved by me.

She floats upon the river of his thoughts.

Like, —but oh how different!

> O woman! in our hours of ease,
> Uncertain, coy, and hard to please,
> And variable as the shade
> By the light quivering aspen made;
> When pain and anguish wring the brow,
> A ministering angel thou!

There is in every true woman's heart a spark of heavenly fire, which lies dormant in broad daylight of prosperity; but which kindles up, and beams and blazes in the dark hour of adversity.

> True love is like a firefly bright,
> It glistens best in darkest night.
> In times of peace it burns the same.
> Disaster fans it into flame.

He, from whose lips divine persuasion flows.

> Down on your knees,
> And thank God, fasting, for a good man's love.

Being a husband is a whole-time job.

Some pray to marry the man they love,
My prayer will somewhat vary;
I humbly pray to God above
That I love the man I marry.

To offer a man friendship when love is in his heart is like giving a loaf of bread to one who is dying of thirst.

Believe me, if all those endearing young charms
Which I gaze on so fondly today,
Were to change by tomorrow and fleet in my arms,
Like fairy gifts fading away,
Thou would'st still be adored as this moment
    thou art,
Let thy loveliness fade as it will,
And around the dear ruin each wish of my heart
Would entwine itself verdantly still.

No, the heart that has truly loved never forgets
But as truly loves on to the close;
As the sunflower turns on her god, when he sets,
The same look which she turned when he rose.

I think true love is never blind,
But rather brings an added light,
An inner vision quick to find
The beauties hid from common sight.

An obedient wife is one who obeys her husband when he tells her to do as she pleases.

If she rules him, she never shows she rules.

He for God only, she for God in him.

Oh, there are many things that women know,
That no one tells them, no one needs to tell;
And that they know, their dearest never guess!

Never believe her love is blind,
All his faults are locked securely
In a closet of her mind.

As unto the bow the cord is,
So unto the man is woman,
Though she bends him, she obeys him,
Though she draws him, yet she follows,
Useless each without the other!

What fond and wayward thoughts will slide
Into a lover's head!
"O, mercy!" to myself I cried,
"If Lucy should be dead!"

Where we love is home,
Home that our feet may leave but not our hearts.

Stay, stay at home, my heart and rest;
Home-keeping hearts are happiest.

A good marriage is that in which each appoints the other guardian of his solitude.

Love that should help you to live,
Song that should spur you to soar!

The love of the young for the young is the beginning of living.

They seem to walk on wings, and tread in air.

Two souls with but a single thought,
Two hearts that beat as one.

Like a baby believes in a sandman
With a faith that we can't understand—
Just like children believe in the story
Of Alice in Wonderland!
Like a real pal believes in a comrade
With a friendship that's lasting and true—
Like my Daddy believes in my Mother,
That's how I believe in you!

The love of the old for the old is the beginning of living forever.

Nothing is more beautiful than the love that has weathered the storms of life.

Companioned years have made them comprehend
The comradeship that lies behind a kiss.
The young ask much of life—they ask but this,
To fare the road together to its end.

To me, dear one, you never can be old.
For as you were when first your eye I saw
Such seems your beauty still.

On Valentine's Day (sent in 1928)—

I have no heart to give you,
For I would have you know
The only heart I ever had,
I gave you long ago.

I like not only to be loved, but also to be told that I am loved. And I shall tell you now that to me you are very dear.

None shall part us from each other,
One in life and death are we:
All in all to one another—
I to you and you to me!
You the tree and I the flower—
You the idol; I the throng—
You the day and I the hour—
You the singer; I the song!

How vast a memory has Love!

In bonds of love united, man and wife,
Long, yet too short, they spent a happy life.

Our two souls therefore, which are one,
Though I must go, endure not yet
A breach, but an expansion,
Like gold to airy thinness beat.

If I shouldn't be around
When the robins come,
Give the one in red cravat
A memorial crumb.

Love like ours can never die.

When we at death must part,
Not like the world's our pain;
But one in Christ and one in heart,
We part to meet again.

Until we meet again before God's throne,
Clothed in the spotless robe He gives His own,
Until we know even as we are known—
Good-night!

Dear Lord, I thank You for the love that, looking through the shadows, sees that You and he and I are ever one!

Joy

Talk happiness.
The world is sad enough
Without your woe.
No path is wholly rough.

If solid happiness we prize,
Within our breast this jewel lies,
And they are fools who roam.
The world has nothing to bestow;
From our own selves our joys must flow,
And that dear hut, our home.

Worth seeing? Yes, but not worth going to see.

Imagination is as good as many voyages—and how much cheaper.

The hours we pass with happy prospects in view are more pleasing than those crowned with fruition.

Sunrise and sunset occur every day, but few ever see them.

I remember, I remember
The fir-trees dark and high;
I used to think their slender tops
Were close against the sky:
It was a childish ignorance,
But now 'tis little joy
To know I'm farther off from heaven
Than when I was a boy.

I remember, I remember
The house where I was born,
The little window where the sun
Came peeping in at morn.
He never came a wink too soon
Nor brought too long a day.

Happiness depends, as you well know
Less on exterior things than most suppose.

My heart leaps up when I behold
A rainbow in the sky . . . .
So was it when my life began;
So is it now I am a man.

Travel on life's common way in cheerful godliness.

A man he seems of cheerful yesterdays and confident tomorrows.

If you of fortune be bereft
And in your store there be but left
Two loaves, sell one and with the dole
Buy hyacinths to feed your soul.

Some feelings are to mortals given,
With less of earth in them than heaven.

Not many sounds in life exceed in interest a knock at the door.

Doorbells are like a magic game,
Or the grab-bag at a fair—
You may never know when you hear one ring
Who may be waiting there.

I never crossed your threshold with a grief
But that I went without it.

No man can feel himself alone
The while he bravely stands
Between the best friends ever known—
His two good, honest hands.

How happy is he born and taught,
That serves not another's will;
Whose armour is his honest thought,
And simple truth his utmost skill!

Lord of himself, though not of lands;
And having nothing, yet has all.

Be your own palace or the world is your jail.

We are here to add what we can *to,* not get what we can *from* life.

No use to grumble and complain,
It's just as easy to rejoice.

Rejoice evermore.
1 Thessalonians 5:16

Rejoice in the Lord alway: and again I say, Rejoice.
Philippians 4:4

When God sorts out the weather and sends rain,
Why rain's my choice.

There is no season such delight can bring,
As summer, autumn, winter, and the spring.

My joy, my grief, my hope, my love,
Did all within this circle move.

The world is so full of a number of things
I'm sure we should all be as happy as kings.

It's easy enough to titter
When the stew is smokin' hot,
But it's mighty hard to giggle
When there's nothin' in the pot.

All are not merry who dance lightly.

Where there is sorrow, there is holy ground.

Sighed one at the end of a harried day: "I heard a bit of good news today—we shall pass this way but once."

A thing is important if you think it is important.

For years and years together
You may be blessed with the sunniest weather.
But in a moment—Presto!—Pass!
Your joys are withered like the grass.

> In the day of prosperity be joyful, but in the day of adversity consider: God also hath set the one over against the other, to the end that man should find nothing after him.
> Ecclesiastes 7:14

If the world's a vale of tears,
Smile, till rainbows span it!

As sorrowful, yet alway rejoicing . . . .
2 Corinthians 6:10

I do not own an inch of land,
But all I see is mine.

Exhilaration is that feeling you get after a great idea hits you and before you realize what's wrong with it.

To burn always with this hard, gemlike flame, to maintain this ecstasy, is success in life.

Those who want fewest things are the happiest.

Resolve to be yourself, and know that he
Who finds himself, loses his misery.

Every joy is gain
And gain is gain, however small.

No longer forward nor behind
I look in hope or fear;
But, grateful, take the good I find,
The best of now and here.

Do you enjoy merry company, or are you seeking to get away from yourself?

Patch grief with proverbs.

Find tongues in trees, books in the running
brooks,
Sermons in stones, and good in everything.

I am the heir of all the ages!

The whole world seems to smile upon me.

There is no house like God's out-of-doors.

The supreme happiness of life is the conviction that we are loved by God Himself.

> . . . even the very hairs of your head are all numbered . . . .
>
> Luke 12:7

Every flower seems to enjoy the air it breathes.

Now or never is the time!

Tomorrow—oh 'twill never be,
If we should live a thousand years!
Our time is all today, today.

> . . . exhort one another daily, while it is called To day; lest any of you be hardened through the deceitfulness of sin.
>
> Hebrews 3:13

Today is the day of salvation!

We know nothing of tomorrow; our business is to be good and happy today.

The rule of joy and the law of duty seems to me all one.

Not what we have, but what we use;
Not what we see, but what we choose—
These are the things that mar or bless
The sum of human happiness.

Worldliness, revelry and high life are not the road to happiness.

Brown bread and the Gospel are good fare.

Enjoy yourself.

Enjoy the friendship and conversation of a few select friends.

> My mind to me an empire is
> While God gives me health.

Every tooth in a man's head is worth more than a diamond.

True happiness consists not in a multitude of friends, but in the worth and choice.

Good company in a journey makes the way to seem the shorter.

> It was only a glad "Good morning,"
> As she passed along the way,
> But it spread the morning's glory
> Over the livelong day.

Every estate is happy if he that bears it is content.

Where the willingness is great, the difficulties cannot be great.

> A mind not to be changed by place or time—
> The mind is its own place and in itself
> Can make a heaven of hell, a hell of heaven.

Nothing is miserable but what is thought so.

I feel good when I feel bad, for I know how good I'll feel when I feel good again.

All joys I bless, but I confess
There is one greatest thrill—
What the Dentist does when he stops the buzz
And puts away the drill.

Unless it be the exhilaration that comes from being shot at and not hit!

Nothing except a battle lost can be half so melancholy as a battle won.

It is better to live rich than to die rich.

Whatever prosperous hour Providence bestows upon you, receive it with a thankful hand; and defer not the enjoyment of the comforts of life.

> Go thy way, eat thy bread with joy, and drink thy wine with a merry heart; for God now accepteth thy works.
>
> Ecclesiastes 9:7

O how sweet it is, this life we live and see!

Joy is the thanks we say to God.

The music in my heart I bore
Long after it was heard no more.

There is delight in singing, though none hears but the singer.

Singing is twice praying.

Life is painting a picture.

In the faces of people, I see God!

He has a daily beauty in his life.

I have heard the chimes at midnight!

Happiness is like time and space—we make and measure it ourselves—as big, as little, as we please.

Our hope is ever livelier than despair, our joy livelier and more abiding than our sorrows are.

He cheered up himself with ends of verse and sayings of philosophers.

We carry with us the wonders we seek without us.

If God wanted us to see the sunrise, He would have had it come up later in the day.

Sometimes the new friends
Leave the heart aglow,
But it's when they're like the ones
We cherished long ago.

I love the Christmastide, and yet,
I notice this, each year I live;
I always like the gifts I get,
But how I love the gifts I give!

I benefit myself in aiding you.

Do not expect something for nothing.

It is our duty to love even those who wrong us.

> Joy to forgive and joy to be forgiven
> Hang level in the balance of Love.

> My dear Christian men, be sure
> Wealth or rank possessing;
> Ye who now do bless the poor
> Shall yourselves find blessing.

Labor disgraces no man; unfortunately you occasionally find men who disgrace labor.

> To look up and not down,
> To look forward and not back,
> To look out and not in, and
> To lend a hand.

What men call treasure God calls dross.

> . . . I count all things but loss for the excellency of the knowledge of Christ Jesus my Lord: for whom I have suffered the loss of all things, and do count them but dung, that I may win Christ.
>
> Philippians 3:8

> Sad soul, take comfort, nor forget
> That sunrise never failed us yet.

The spirit of truth and the spirit of freedom—they are the pillars of society.

There can be no freedom or beauty about a home life that depends on borrowing and debt.

'Tis distance robes the mountain in its azure hue.

Pain and boredom are two foes of human happiness.

> 'Tis not the meat, but 'tis the appetite
> Makes eating a delight.

You never miss the water till the well runs dry.

There is no music in a rest, but there is the making of music in it. Miss not that part of the life-melody.

God Almighty first planted a garden.

God be praised! To believing souls He gives light in darkness, comfort in despair!

This is good enough to be true!

A smile cannot be bought, begged, borrowed, or stolen, for it is something that is no good to anybody until it is given away.

The rich need a smile and the poor are richer when they receive it.

A smile enriches those who receive it without diminishing the supply of the giver.

There is no beautifier of the face like the wish to scatter joy abroad.

Learn the sweet magic of a cheerful face;
Not always smiling, but at least serene.

If you hear a song that thrills you,
Sung by any child of song,
Praise it. Do not let the singer
Wait deserved praises long.
Why should one who thrills your heart
Lack the joy you may impart?

There is a time when silence is more musical than any song.

Happy is the house that shelters a friend.

Since every day by God we live,
May grateful hearts His gifts receive;
And may the hands be pure from stain
With which our daily bread we gain.

The year with good God crowns,
The earth His mercy fills,
The wilderness is fruitful,
And joyful are the hills;
With corn the vales are covered,
The flocks in pastures graze;
All nature joins in singing
A joyful song of praise.

Earth with her thousand voices praises God.

Morning, evening, noon and night, Praise God!

The desire of knowledge increases ever with the acquisition of it.

Writing is but a different name for conversation.

Live always in the best company when you read.

Nimble thought can jump both sea and land.

> . . . blessed are they that hear the word of God, and keep it.
>
> Luke 11:28

> Thy testimonies have I taken as an heritage for ever: for they are the rejoicing of my heart.
>
> Psalms 119:111

> Thy statutes have been my songs . . . .
>
> Psalms 119:54

> Thy testimonies also are my delight and my counsellors.
>
> Psalms 119:24

> . . . I will delight myself in thy commandments, which I have loved.
>
> Psalms 119:47

He ate and drank the precious words,
His spirit grew robust;
He knew no more that he was poor,
Nor that his frame was dust.

He danced along the dingy days,
And this bequest of wings
Was but a book. What liberty
A loosened spirit brings!

It had to be *The Book!*

This is throw-your-hat-into-the-air time!

Work

Blessed is he who has found his work; let him seek no other blessedness.

Do you love life? Then do not squander time, for that is the stuff life is made of.

Mingle your joys with your earnest occupation.

The sun gives light as soon as it rises.

Give to the world the best you have,
And the best will come back to you.

. . . he which soweth bountifully shall reap also bountifully.

2 Corinthians 9:6

Plough deep while sluggards sleep.

Never leave that till tomorrow which you can do today.

All work is as seed sown; it grows and spreads, and sows itself anew.

Work brings its own relief;
He who most idle is
Has most of grief.

He who makes a garden
Works hand-in-hand with God.

There is nothing so easy but that it becomes difficult when you do it with reluctance.

. . . whatsoever ye do, do it heartily, as to the Lord, and not unto men.

Colossians 3:23

Enough work to do, and strength enough to do the work.

He has half the deed done
Who has made a beginning.

Let each man pass his days in that wherein his skill is greatest.

He lives twice who can at once employ
The present well, and even the past enjoy.

There is no substitute for hard work.

Time is the most valuable thing you can spend.

Nothing is so dear and precious as time.

A fair day's wages for a fair day's work—the everlasting right of man.

A fair little girl sat under a tree,
Sewing as long as her eyes could see;
She smoothed her work, and folded it right,
And said, "Dear work, good-night, good-night."

All work is noble.

All service ranks the same with God.

If time be heavy on your hands,
Are there no beggars at your gate,
Nor any poor about your lands?
Oh! teach the orphan boy to read,
Or teach the orphan girl to sew.

There are those who toil for the spiritually indispensable; not daily bread, but the bread of life.

. . . Man shall not live by bread alone, but by every word that proceedeth out of the mouth of God.

Matthew 4:4

Work consists of whatever a body is obliged to do.

Play consists of whatever a body is not obliged to do.

Thank God every morning when you get up that you have something to do that day which must be done, whether you like it or not. Being forced to work, and forced to do your best, will breed in you temperance and self-control, diligence, and strength of will, cheerfulness and content, and many virtues which the idle never know.

There is always work,
And tools to work withal, for those who will;
And blessed are the horny hands of toil.

To lift up the hands in prayer gives God glory, but a man with a dungfork in his hand, a woman with a slop-pail, give Him glory too. He is so great that all things give Him glory if you mean they should!

This is my work; my blessing, not my doom;
Of all who live, I am the one by whom
This work can best be done in the right way.

Genius does what it must, and talent what it can.

Men of genius do not excel in any profession because they labor in it, but they labor in it because they excel.

There is no better ballast for keeping the mind steady on its keel, and saving it from all risk of crankiness, than business.

When men are rightly occupied, their amusement grows out of their work.

To business that we love we rise and go to it with delight.

Hard work results in rest for the body and peace to the mind.

The beginning is the most important part of the work.

God forbid that I should ever be at leisure.

Being in a hurry is one of the tributes we pay to life.

God is not willing to do everything and thus take away our free will and the share of glory which belongs to us.

Time and tide wait for no man.

Make hay while the sun shines.

> Go to the ant, thou sluggard; consider her ways, and be wise: Which having no guide, overseer, or ruler, Provideth her meat in the summer, and gathereth her food in the harvest.
>
> Proverbs 6:6–8

Hold every moment sacred. Give each clarity and meaning, each the weight of your awareness, each its true and due fulfilment.

Are you little? Do your little well,
And for your comfort know:
The biggest man can do his biggest work
No better than just so.

When I did my best at a job, my mother would say, "That's all a mule could do."

I have many a voice that is loud and strong
To speak to the world for Me.
But I've no one to sing a lullaby song
To this wee little babe but thee.

The vocation of every man and woman is to serve other people.

Dear Lord,
Help me, that I may never shirk,
But always look upon my work
As coming, Lord, from Thee;
And may, in doing well my part,
This holy thought, inspire my heart—
You, Father, sent to me!

. . . My Father worketh hitherto, and I work.
John 5:17

■

Peace

Be your own home, and in yourself dwell.

> Within my earthly temple there's a crowd.
> There's one of us that's humble; one that's proud.
> There's one that's broken-hearted for his sins,
> And one who, unrepentant, sits and grins.
> There's one who loves his neighbor as himself,
> And one who cares for naught but fame and pelf.
> From much corroding care would I be free
> If once I could determine which is Me.

. . . the good that I would I do not: but the evil which I would not, that I do. O wretched man that I am! . . . .
Romans 7:19, 24

To sit alone with my conscience will be judgment enough for me.

Let us not burden our remembrances with a heaviness that's gone.

And there is even a happiness that makes the heart afraid.

May I busy myself with confessing my own sins and leave yours for you to confess.

Do your own job well, and let the other fellow take care of his.

The thing of which I have most fear is fear.

Worry is the interest paid by those who borrow trouble.

It is worse to be soul-hungry than body-hungry.

We are wanderers between two worlds—hence our discontent.

There comes an hour of sadness
With the setting of the sun,
Not for sins committed,
But for things I have not done.

Am I content in pleasing my Lord only?

The bow too tensely strung is easily broken.

He had a face like a benediction.

She is shut in with measureless content.

The peace above all—a still and quiet conscience.

Where the stream runs smoothest, the water is deepest.

The quiet mind is richer than a crown.

He is well paid that is well satisfied.

Poor and content is rich, and rich enough.

Tension is driving with the brakes on.

> When from our better selves we have too long
> Been parted by the hurrying world, and droop,
> Sick of its business, of its pleasures tired,
> How gracious, how benign, is Solitude.

When you have shut your doors, and darkened your room, remember never to say that you are alone, for you are not alone; but God is within, and your genius is within—and what need have they of light to see what you are doing?

> Companion none is like
> Unto the mind alone;
> For many have been harmed by speech,
> Through thinking, few or none.

> I have heard songs in the Silence
> That shall never float into speech.

Of all the words the Evangelists record,
To comfort souls perplexed and distressed,
This ever seems to me divinest, best—
The thought that Peter spoke—
"Thou knowest, Lord."

Do all things without murmurings and disputings: That ye may be blameless and harmless, the sons of God, without rebuke, in the midst of a crooked and perverse nation, among whom ye shine as lights in the world; Holding forth the word of life . . . .

Philippians 2:14–16

He makes a solitude, and calls it—peace!

How sweet, how passing sweet, is solitude!
But grant me still a friend in my retreat,
To whom I may whisper, Solitude is sweet.

Let your boat of life be lightly packed with only what you need.

Those who have steeped their souls in prayer
Can every anguish calmly bear.

A Garden is a lovesome thing, God knows!
Rose plot,
Fringed pool,
Ferned pot—
The veriest school
Of Peace; and yet the fool

Contends that God is not—
Not God! in Gardens! when the eve is cool?
Nay, but I have a sign:
'Tis very sure God walks in mine.

Ah! when shall all men's good
Be each man's rule, and universal peace
Lie like a shaft of light across the land?

There is always a comforting thought in time of trouble, when it is not our trouble.

The holiest of all holidays are those
Kept by ourselves in silence and apart;
The secret anniversaries of the heart.

Peace and rest at length have come,
All the day's long toil is past,
And each heart is whispering, "Home,
Home at last."

Of all the thoughts of God that are
Borne inward into souls afar,
Along the Psalmist's music deep,
Now tell me if that any is,
For gift of grace, surpassing this:
"He giveth his beloved—sleep."

It is vain for you to rise up early, to sit up late, to eat the bread of sorrows: for so he giveth his beloved sleep.

Psalms 127:2

O bed! O bed! delicious bed!
That heaven upon earth to the weary head!

The sleep of a labouring man is sweet, whether he eat little or much: but the abundance of the rich will not suffer him to sleep.

Ecclesiastes 5:12

Sweet are the slumbers of the virtuous man.

There's nothing, nothing, nothing, I say,
That's worth the lying awake!

When upon life's billows you are tempest tossed,
When you are discouraged, thinking all is lost,
Count your many blessings, name them one by one.
And it will surprise you what the Lord hath done.

Now I lay me down to sleep,
I pray the Lord my soul to keep;
If I should die before I wake,
I pray the Lord my soul to take.

Old Age

It is time to be old—to take in sail.

> For age is opportunity no less
> Than youth itself, though in another dress,
> And as the evening twilight fades away
> The sky is filled with stars, invisible by day.

> And silence, like a poultice, comes
> To heal the blows of sound.

It matters not how long you live, but how well.

We live in deeds, not years; in thoughts, not breaths.

I'm growing fonder of my staff;
I'm growing dimmer in my eyes;
I'm growing fainter in my laugh;
I'm growing deeper in my sighs;
I'm growing careless of my dress;
I'm growing frugal of my gold;
I'm growing wise; I'm growing—yes—
I'm growing old!

So precious life is! Even to the old
The hours are as a miser's coins!

To be seventy years young is sometimes far more cheerful and hopeful than to be forty years old.

Three-score summers, when they're gone,
Will appear as short as one.

Time has laid his hand
Upon my heart, gently, not smiting it,
But as a harper lays his open palm
Upon his harp to deaden its vibrations.

What though youth gave love and roses,
Age still leaves us friends and wine—
And memories, precious memories!

If life had a second edition, how I would correct the proofs! Yes and no. I would not make some of the same mistakes over, but I'm pretty sure I'd come up with some new ones.

My age is as a lusty winter,
Frosty, but kindly.

With years a richer life begins,
The spirit mellows:
Ripe age gives tone to violins,
Wine, and good fellows.

Youth should heed the older-witted
When they say, don't go too far—
Now their sins are all committed,
Lord, how virtuous they are!

Time goes, you say? Ah no!
Alas, Time stays, we go.

My feet are heavy now but on I go,
My head erect beneath the waning years.

How noiseless falls the foot of time!

We're tired, my heart and I.

I am declined
Into the vale of years.

Every day should be passed as if it were our last.

The good man prolongs his life; to be able to enjoy one's past life is to live twice.

Come to your old age like the setting sun, of which the grandeur remains, though not the intensity.

Great peace have they which love thy law: and nothing shall offend them.

Psalms 119:165

Speaking of King David and King Solomon—
When old age crept over them
With many, many qualms,
King Solomon wrote the Proverbs
And King David wrote the Psalms.

I grow old learning something new every day.

When grace is joined with wrinkles, it is adorable.

Lives of great men all remind us
We can make our lives sublime,
And, departing, leave behind us
Footprints on the sands of time.

Let not your mind grow torpid from want of use in old age.

Enlarge my life with multitude of days,
In health, in sickness, thus the suppliant prays;
Hides from himself his state, and shuns to know
That life protracted is protracted woe.

Care to our coffin adds a nail, no doubt,
And every grin so merry draws one out.

. . . though our outward man perish, yet the inward man is renewed day by day.

2 Corinthians 4:16

Build you more stately mansions, O my soul,
As the swift seasons roll!
Leave your low-vaulted past!
Let each new temple be nobler than the last!

I see not a step before me
as I tread on another year;
But I've left the Past in God's keeping—
The Future His mercy shall clear;
And what looks dark in the distance,
May brighten as I draw near.

Serene, I fold my hands and wait,
Nor care for wind, nor tide, nor sea;
I rave no more 'gainst time or fate,
For lo! my own shall come to me.

Memory is the diary that we all carry about with us.

. . . an old age serene and bright,
And lovely as a starry night,
Shall lead you to your grave.

Thus aged men, full loth and slow,
The vanities of life forego,
And count their youthful follies o'er
Till Memory lends her light no more.

I cannot sing the old songs now!
It is not that I deem them low;
'Tis that I can't remember how they go.

Cold the stars are, cold the earth is,
Everything is grim and cold!
Strange and drear the sound of mirth is
—Life and I are old.

Noise is the most impertinent of all forms of interruption. It is not only an interruption, but also a disruption of thought.

Time as he grows old teaches many lessons.

Old age is a second childhood.

The harvest of old age is time to reflect and count our blessings—past and present.

A tranquil mind is a mind well ordered.

. . . the sunless pleasures of weary people, whose care for external things is slackening.

I am tired of tears and laughter,
And men that laugh and weep;
Of what may come hereafter
For men that sow and reap:
I am weary of days and hours,
Blown buds of barren flowers,
Desires and dreams and powers
And everything but sleep.

It is like stirring living embers when, at eighty, one remembers all the achings and the quakings of the times that try men's souls.

Age, like distance, lends a double charm.

And still to love, though prest with ill,
In wintry age to feel no chill,
With me is to be lovely still,
My Mary!

If peace and quietness are not in your power, give yourself bodily fatigue.

'Tis the last rose of summer,
Left blooming alone;
All her lovely companions
Are faded and gone;
No flower of her kindred,
No rosebud is nigh,
To reflect back her blushes,
Or give sigh for sigh.

Her soul saw a glimpse of happiness through the chinks of her sickness-broken body.

I know—yet my arms are empty,
That fondly folded seven.
And the mother-heart within me
Is almost starved for heaven.

When I remember by-gone days
I think how evening follows morn;
So many I loved were not yet dead,
So many I love were not yet born.

The same old charitable lie
Repeated as the years scoot by
Perpetually makes a hit—
"You really haven't changed a bit!"

As a white candle
In a holy place
So is the beauty
Of an aged face.

Youth, large, lusty, living Youth,
Full of grace, force, and fascination,
Do you know that Old Age may come after you,
With equal grace, force, fascination?

The dweller in my "house" is young and bright and gay;
Just starting on a life to last throughout eternal day.
You only see the outside, which is all that most folk see.
Don't mix my "house" with "me."

Do your joys with age diminish?
When mine fail me, I'll complain.

Say what you will, the young are never happy—they have not lived long enough. Give me blessed Age, beyond the fire and fever!

As we grow older, we see deeper into the beauty, the joy and the sadness of life.

Did you ever hear your grandmother talk to herself when she was alone? No, I was never with her when she was alone.

The years seem to rush by now, and I think of death as a fast approaching end of a journey—double and treble reason for loving, as well as working, while it is day.

> An aged man is but a paltry thing
> A tattered coat upon a stick, unless
> Soul clap its hands and sing . . .
> For every tatter in its mortal dress.

The older a person gets, the noisier children are.

> And there is the silence of age,
> Too full of wisdom for the tongue to utter it
> In words intelligible to those who have not lived
> The great range of life.

Life is a highway, and its milestones are the years.

> So may you live, till like ripe fruit, you drop
> Into your mother's lap, or be with ease
> Gathered, not harshly plucked, for death mature.
> This is old age.

Patience

Who breathes, must suffer, and who thinks must mourn.

For whom the Lord loveth he chasteneth, and scourgeth every son whom he receiveth.

Hebrews 12:6

God is not always angry when He strikes,
But most chastises those whom most He likes.

David's Psalms had ne'er been sung
If grief his heart had never wrung.

To be resigned when ills betide,
Patient when favors are denied,
And pleased with favors given—
Dear child, this is wisdom's part;
This is the incense of the heart
Whose fragrance smells to heaven.

Genius is nothing but an aptitude for patience.

And this, too, shall pass away.

Be not of that number who are ignorant in spite of experience.

Experience keeps a dear school, and Fools will learn in no other.

I can tell where my own shoe pinches me.

Can anybody remember when the times were not hard and money scarce?

The heights by great men reached and kept
Were not attained by sudden flight.
But they, while their companions slept,
Were toiling upward in the night.

Happiness is produced not so much by great pieces of good fortune that seldom happen, as by little advantages that occur every day.

It takes a long time to bring excellence to maturity.

Mishaps are like knives, that either serve us or cut us, as we grasp them by the blade or the handle.

But the rose with all its thorns excels all other flowers.

The Future is something which everyone reaches at the rate of sixty minutes an hour, whatever he does, whoever he is.

O how full of briars is this working-day world!

Success is failure turned inside out.

Yield not to misfortunes, but press forward the more boldly in their face.

Fire is the test of gold; adversity of strong men.

Watch for your opportunity.

We would often be sorry if our wishes were gratified.

The little reed, bending to the force of the wind, soon stood upright again when the storm had passed over.

Circumstances alter cases.

The worst men often give the best advice.

On the 32nd day of the 13th month
  Of the 8th day of the week,
On the 25th hour and the 61st minute,
  We'll find all that we seek.

(For we walk by faith, not by sight).
2 Corinthians 5:7

Others' follies teach us not,
Nor much their wisdom teaches;
And most, of sterling worth, is what
Our own experience preaches.

Root, hog, or die!

Life is too short to waste
In critic peep or cynic bark,
Quarrel or reprimand:
'Twill soon be dark;
Up! mind your own aim, and
God speed the mark!

Do a thing incomparably well and the public will beat a path to your door, even though you live in a forest.

While pensive poets painful vigils keep,
Sleepless themselves to give their readers sleep.

Nothing begins, and nothing ends,
That is not paid with moan;
For we are born in other's pain,
And perish in our own.

Oh, a trouble's a ton, or a trouble's an ounce,
Or a trouble is what you make it,
And it isn't the fact that you're hurt that counts,
But only how did you take it?

If nobody knows the troubles you've seen, you don't live in a small town.

When care is pressing you down a bit,
Rest, if you must, but don't quit.

Don't give up, though the pace seems slow—
You might succeed with just one more blow.

Stick to the fight when you are hardest hit—
It's when things seem worst that you must not quit.

The good are better made by ill,
As odors crushed are sweeter still.

Superfluous branches
We lop away, that bearing boughs may live.

I [Jesus] am the true vine, and my Father is the husbandman. Every branch in me that beareth not fruit he taketh away: and every branch that beareth fruit, he purgeth it, that it may bring forth more fruit.

John 15:1, 2

There is no good in arguing with the inevitable. The only argument available with an east wind is to put on your overcoat.

It is good for me that I have been afflicted; that I might learn thy statutes.

Psalms 119:71

Who never ate his bread in sorrow,
Who never spent the darksome hours
Weeping; and watching for the morrow—
He knows You not, Ye Heavenly Powers.

One woe seems to tread upon another's heel,
So fast they follow.

Come what, come may,
Time and the hour run
Through the roughest day.

The way to bliss lies not on beds of down,
And he that has no cross deserves no crown.

Come unto me [Jesus], all ye that labour and are heavy laden, and I will give you rest. Take my yoke upon you, and learn of me; for I am meek and lowly in heart: and ye shall find rest unto your souls. For my yoke is easy, and my burden is light.

Matthew 11:28–30

By suffering comes wisdom.

Patience is the best remedy for every trouble.

Anyone can hold the helm when the sea is calm.

On the strength of one link in the cable
Depends the might of the chain:
Who knows when you may be tested?
So live that you bear the strain.

Doing what's right is no guarantee against misfortune.

Don't be discouraged. It may be the last key in the bunch that will open the door.

A minute of success pays for the failure of years.

Take a long view of success.

Take opportunity or make opportunity.

We learn in suffering what we teach in song.

> We look before and after,
> And pine for what is not;
> Our sincerest laughter
> With some pain is fraught;
> Our sweetest songs are those that tell
> of saddest thought.

> I received a secret wound—
> But the wound grew a pearl at last.

When life is more terrible than death, it is then the truest valor to dare to live.

From our own we learn to melt at another's woes.

If Winter comes, can Spring be far behind?

Just about everything happens to everybody, sooner or later.

> Many strokes, though with a little axe,
> Hew down and fell the hardest-timbered oaks.

Experience can be a jewel.

How poor are they who have not patience!

Only a few seem capable of education: teach as you will, only a few will profit by your most zealous energy.

There are none so blind as those who will not see.

> . . . O foolish people, and without understanding; which have eyes, and see not; which have ears, and hear not.
> Jeremiah 5:21

There's not the least that can be said or done, but people will talk and find fault.

Men disappoint me so, but no more than I disappoint myself.

A sure way to be popular is to listen closely to things you already know.

It is only one step from toleration to forgiveness.

The wheel that squeaks the loudest
Is the one that gets the grease.

Better a little chiding now than a great deal of heartbreak later.

Can you look into the seeds of time
And say which grain will grow and which will not?

The worst way to improve the world is to condemn it.

No man can justly censure or condemn another, because indeed no man truly knows another.

You cannot put the same shoe on every foot.

It is better to learn late than never.

I believe she would make three bites of a cherry.

We are almost as alike as eggs.

Take the good will for the deed.

Charm agony with words.

A friend should bear his friend's infirmities.

We shall have as weak and as strong, as silly and as wise, as bad and as good men with us always, I suppose.

> Of all the horrid, hideous notes of woe,
> I detest more, "I told you so."

The chief purpose of virtue is to bear with patience the injustice of our fellows.

> Do not pray for tasks equal to your powers.
> Pray for powers equal to your tasks.

> But they that wait upon the Lord shall renew their strength; they shall mount up with wings as eagles; they shall run, and not be weary; and they shall walk, and not faint.
>
> Isaiah 40:31

Time tries the truth in everything.

Experience is the name we give to our mistakes.

It takes a heap of livin' in a house t' make it home,
A heap o' sun an' shadder, an' ye sometimes have t' roam
Afore ye really 'preciate the things ye lef' behind,
An' hunger fer 'em somehow, with 'em allus on yer mind.

Each is given a bag of tools,
A shapeless mass,
A book of rules;
And each must make,
Ere life is flown,
A stumbling block
Or a stepping stone.

Many small make a great.

None knows the weight of another's burden.

Bear ye one another's burdens, and so fulfil the law of Christ . . . . every man shall bear his own burden.
Galatians 6:2, 5

Casting all your care upon him [God]; for he careth for you.
1 Peter 5:7

Practice is the best of all instructors.

Practice makes perfect.

Things are not always what they seem.

A continual dropping wears away a stone.

Courage is to feel
The daily daggers of relentless steel
And keep on living.

Are you the topmost apple
The gatherers could not reach,
Reddening on the bough?

God still speaks to those who take time to listen.

They do me [opportunity] wrong who say I come no more
When once I knock and fail to find you in;
For every day I stand outside your door
And bid you wake, and rise to fight and win.

God's mercy endures for ever!

■

Goodness

I owe the land in which I live the morality of my actions and the love of virtue.

> That for which all virtue now is sold
> And almost every vice is almighty gold.

For the love of money is the root of all evil: which while some coveted after, they have erred from the faith, and pierced themselves through with many sorrows.

1 Timothy 6:10

Virtue and riches seldom settle on one man.

> . . . Jesus . . . saith unto them, Children, how hard is it for them that trust in riches to enter into the kingdom of God!
>
> Mark 10:24

Love Virtue, she alone is free,
She can teach you how to climb
Higher than the sphery chime;
Or, if Virtue feeble were,
Heaven itself would stoop to her.

Virtue is sufficient of herself for happiness.

Virtue is its own reward.

There is no higher ideal for man and of virtue than the ideal given us by Christ.

I was shipwrecked before I got aboard.

> He that saith he abideth in him [Jesus] ought himself also so to walk, even as he walked.
>
> 1 John 2:6

In vain we call old notions fudge,
And bend our conscience to our dealing;
The Ten Commandments will not budge,
And stealing will continue stealing.

> Wherewithal shall a young man cleanse his way? by taking heed thereto according to thy word.
>
> Psalms 119:9

Being born again, not of corruptible seed, but of incorruptible, by the word of God, which liveth and abideth for ever.

1 Peter 1:23

Thy word have I hid in mine heart, that I might not sin against thee.

Psalms 119:11

He that is of God heareth God's words: ye therefore hear them not, because ye are not of God.

John 8:47

Confession of our faults is the next thing to innocency.

It matters not what you are thought to be, but what you are.

What you are thunders so loud that I cannot hear what you say.

Who to himself is law no law needs.

A man of worth in his own household will appear upright in the state also.

Where there is no free agency, there can be no morality.

Where there is not temptation, there can be little claim to virtue.

There's many a life of sweet content
Whose virtue is environment.

When the routine is rigorously condemned by law, the law, and not the man, must have the credit of the conduct.

> . . . work out your own salvation with fear and trembling.
>
> Philippians 2:12

Education has for its object the formation of character.

Morality knows nothing of geography or race.

I am the inferior of any man whose rights I trample underfoot.

It is not enough to do good; one must do it the right way.

It is quality rather than quantity that matters.

> What can we know? or what can we discern,
> When error chokes the windows of the mind?

Truth is forever truth.

The highest proof of virtue is to possess boundless power without abusing it.

Men should utter nothing for which they would not willingly be responsible through time and in eternity.

Evil is wrought by want of thought, as well as want of heart.

> Straight is the line of Duty,
> Curved is the line of Beauty.

Follow the straight line, you shall see
The curved line ever follow thee.

The only significance of life consists in helping to establish the kingdom of God; and this can be done only by means of the acknowledgment and profession of the truth by each one of us.

He will hew to the right, let the chips fall where they may.

His Christianity was muscular.

Pay every debt as if God wrote the bill.

Virtue, though in rags, will keep me warm.

Hard was their lodging, homely was their food;
For all their luxury was doing good.

They are only truly great who are truly good.

Some men do not care how nobly they live, but only how long. It is within the reach of every man to live nobly, but within no man's power to live long.

Selfishness is the greatest curse of the human race.

For himself does a man work evil in working evil for another.

. . . base gains are the same as losses.

If good men were only better,
Would the wicked be so bad?

This learned I from the shadow of a tree,
That to and fro did sway against a wall,
Our shadow selves, our influence, may fall
Where we ourselves can never be.

Truth from his lips prevailed with double sway
And fools, who came to scoff, remained to pray.

More people are flattered into virtue than bullied out of vice.

Example is the best precept.

He who should teach men to die would at the same time teach them to live.

By the work one knows the workman.

The belief in a supernatural source of evil is not necessary; men alone are quite capable of every wickedness of sin!

O the ugliness, the vileness, the awfulness, the wickedness of sin!

Vice is a monster of so frightful mien,
As to be hated needs but to be seen;
Yet seen too oft, familiar with her face,
We first endure, then pity, then embrace.

Woe unto them that draw iniquity with cords of vanity, and sin as it were with a cart rope.

Isaiah 5:18

Easy is the descent to Hell; night and day the gates stand open.

> Enter ye in at the strait gate: for wide is the gate, and broad is the way, that leadeth to destruction, and many there be which go in thereat: Because strait is the gate, and narrow is the way, which leadeth unto life, and few there be that find it.
>
> Matthew 7:13, 14

The heart of man is the place the devils dwell in: I feel sometimes a hell within myself.

To change systems and to change institutions without changing the hearts of men is useless.

Why make good laws for bad people?

That man who lives for self alone
Lives for the meanest mortal known.

The greatest minds are capable of the greatest vices as well as the greatest virtues.

Satan now is wiser than of yore,
And tempts by making rich, not making poor.

Oft has a whole city reaped the evil fruit of a bad man.

A hundred fools do not make one wise man.

Hell is paved with good intentions.

He that lies with the dogs rises with fleas.

A man should be upright, not kept upright.

It is no fault of Christianity if I fall into sin.

Speech is a mirror of the soul: as a man speaks, so is he.

Dare to be true! Nothing can need a lie.

The falsehood of the tongue leads to that of the heart.

What our hearts think, our tongue speaks.

> For as he thinketh in his heart, so is he . . . .
> Proverbs 23:7

Say what you mean and mean what you say.

> He that does one fault at first,
> And lies to hide it, makes it two.

A promise made is a debt unpaid.

A lie may easily get you out of a scrape, but 'twill make you happier to take the scrape and leave out the lie.

An honest man's word is as good as his bond.

If you call a tail a leg, how many legs has a dog? Five? No, calling a tail a leg doesn't make it a leg.

Be ever precise in promise-keeping.

> And though he promise to his loss,
> He makes the promise good.

> Lord . . . who shall dwell in thy holy hill? He that walketh uprightly, and worketh righteousness, and speaketh the truth in his heart. He that backbiteth not with his tongue, nor doeth evil to his neighbour . . . He that sweareth to his own hurt, and changeth not.
>
> Psalms 15:1–4

Small habits well pursued betimes
May reach the degree of crimes.

Tale-bearers are as bad as the tale-makers.

Just as the age 'twixt boy and youth,
When thought is speech and speech is truth.

A lie which is half a truth is ever the blackest of lies. A lie which is all a lie may be met and fought outright, but a lie which is part of a truth is a harder matter to fight.

Repetition of sin is a mockery of repentance.

Look before you leap;
For as you sow, so shall you reap.

> Be not deceived; God is not mocked: for whatsoever a man soweth, that shall he also reap.
>
> Galatians 6:7

Show me the books he loves and I shall know
The man far better than through mortal friends.

The Devil himself is the author of confusion and lies.

. . . he [the devil] is a liar, and the father of it.
John 8:44

Salvation is far from the wicked: for they seek not thy statutes.
Psalms 119:155

To resist him that is set in authority is evil.

. . . Thou shalt not speak evil of the ruler of thy people.
Acts 23:5

Let every soul be subject unto the higher powers. For there is no power but of God: the powers that be are ordained of God. Whosoever therefore resisteth the power, resisteth the ordinance of God: and they that resist shall receive to themselves damnation . . . pay ye tribute also . . . .
Romans 13:1, 2, 6

For modes of faith let graceless zealots fight;
His can't be wrong whose life is in the right.

He is armed without who is innocent within.

His brow is wet with honest sweat,
He earns whate'er he can,
And looks the whole world in the face,
For he owes not any man.

Owe no man any thing, but to love one another: for he that loveth another hath fulfilled the law.
Romans 13:8

The disease of an evil conscience is beyond the practice of all the physicians of all the countries in the world.

O conscience, upright and stainless, how bitter a sting to thee is a little fault!

It is neither safe nor prudent to do aught against conscience.

> . . . the word of God is quick, and powerful, and sharper than any twoedged sword, piercing even to the dividing asunder of soul and spirit, and of the joints and marrow, and is a discerner of the thoughts and intents of the heart.
>
> Hebrews 4:12

National injustice is the surest road to national downfall.

With malice toward none; with charity for all; with firmness in the right, as God gives us to see the right . . . .

I do the very best I know how—the very best I can; and I mean to keep doing so until the end. If the end brings me out all right, what is said against me won't amount to anything. If the end brings me out wrong, ten angels swearing I was right would make no difference.

Virtue is bold, and goodness never fearful.

No legacy is so rich as honesty.

Virtue is like a rich stone—best plain set.

Be noble! and the nobleness that lies
In other men, sleeping but never dead,
Will rise in majesty to meet your own.

The value of good health is next to a good conscience.

Good, the more communicated, more abundant grows.

Remember that virtue is not hereditary.

Gentleness

Life is not so short but that there is always time enough for courtesy.

A little word in kindness spoken,
A motion or a tear,
Has often healed the heart that's broken,
And made a friend sincere.

Then deem it not an idle thing
A pleasant word to speak;
The face you wear—the thoughts you bring—
The heart may heal or break.

Hail, ye small, sweet courtesies of life! for smooth do ye make the road of it.

Teach me to feel another's woe,
To hide the fault I see;
That mercy I to others show,
That mercy show to me.

The ill-timed truth we might have kept—
Who knows how sharp it pierced and stung?
The word we had not sense to say—
Who knows how grandly it had rung?

His words were simple words enough,
And yet he used them so,
That what in other mouths was rough
In his seemed musical and low.

You can tell more about a person by what he says about others than you can by what others say about him.

It is well said again;
And 'tis a kind of good deed to say well:
And yet words are no deeds.

The gentle mind by gentle deeds is known.

How far that little candle throws its beams!
So shines a kind deed in a naughty world.

If you stop to be kind, you must swerve often from your path.

Hold your lighted lamp on high,
Be a star in someone's sky.

The best portion of a good man's life—
His little, nameless, unremembered acts
Of kindness and of love.

She left no little thing behind
Excepting loving thoughts and kind.

She does little kindnesses which most leave undone.

One small candle may light a thousand.

All the beautiful sentiments in the world weigh less than a single lovely action.

I'd rather see a sermon than hear one any day;
I'd rather one should walk with me than merely tell the way.

Example is the school of mankind, and they will learn at no other.

He preaches well that lives well.

Question not, but live and labor
Till your goal be won
Helping every feeble neighbor,
Seeking help from none;
Life is mostly froth and bubble,
Two things stand like stone—
Kindness in another's trouble,
Courage in our own.

Life is a struggle, but not a warfare.

> . . . the servant of the Lord must not strive; but be gentle unto all men, apt to teach, patient.
>
> 2 Timothy 2:24

Good-nature is more agreeable in conversation than wit, and gives a certain air to the countenance which is more admirable than beauty.

Force is no remedy.
Work for some good, be it ever so slowly;
Cherish some flower, be it ever so lowly;
Labor!—all labor is noble and holy!

Let your great deeds be your prayer to God!

It is one thing to show a man that he is in error, and another to put him in possession of truth.

Who will not mercy unto others show,
How can he mercy ever hope to have?

> Blessed are the merciful: for they shall obtain mercy.
>
> Matthew 5:7

A lot of good arguments are spoiled by someone who knows what he's talking about.

A word to the wise is enough.

Who overcomes
By force has overcome but half his foe.

A kindly thing God has made,
His Hand of very healing laid
Upon a fevered world—shade.

Only a cowboy who has ridden under the shade of two telephone wires can truly appreciate shade.

Blow, blow, thou winter wind!
Thou art not so unkind
As man's ingratitude.

Gratitude is the sign of noble souls.

I can no other answer make but thanks,
And thanks, and ever thanks.

She is when unadorned adorned the most.

Handsome is that handsome does.

What's in a name? That which we call a rose
By any other name would smell as sweet.

It hurts not the tongue to give fair words.

Of manners gentle, of affections mild;
In wit a man, simplicity a child.

A child misses the unsaid Goodnight
And falls asleep with heartache.

> But I fear, lest by any means, as the serpent beguiled Eve through his subtilty, so your minds should be corrupted from the simplicity that is in Christ.
>
> 2 Corinthians 11:3

A departure from the simplicity that is in Christ becomes as distinguishable as light from darkness to such who are crucified to the world.

> The lintel is low enough to keep out pomp and pride;
> The threshold high enough to turn deceit aside.

May I in all times and places be a peaceful and sweet companion to my husband.

If there is any kindness I can show, or any good thing I can do, let me do it now.

> Three times I came to your friendly door,
> Three times my shadow was on your floor.
> I was the beggar with bruised feet;
> I was the woman you gave to eat;
> I was the child on the homeless street.

> [Jesus said:] . . . Inasmuch as ye have done it unto one of the least of these my brethren, ye have done it unto me.
>
> Matthew 25:40

Meekness

Humility has a calmness of spirit and a world of other blessings attending upon it.

Humility is the most difficult of all the virtues to achieve; nothing dies harder than the desire to think well of oneself.

Cannot true pride be also humble?

> My soul shall make her boast in the Lord: the humble shall hear thereof, and be glad.
>
> Psalms 34:2

God does not always choose His elect from among the great and wealthy.

> . . . ye see . . . how that not many wise men after the flesh, not many mighty, not many noble, are called: But God hath chosen the foolish things of the world to confound the wise; and God hath chosen the weak things of the world to confound the things which are mighty; And base things of the world, and things which are despised, hath God chosen, yea, and things which are not, to bring to nought things that are: That no flesh should glory in his presence.
>
> 1 Corinthians 1:26–29

That we need God I understand. That He would need me, I cannot comprehend.

A man may fish with the worm that has eaten of a king, and eat of the fish that has fed of the worm.

> The statesman throws his shoulders back, and
> straightens out his tie,
> And says, "My friends, unless it rains, the
> weather will be dry."
> And when the thought into our brain
> has percolated through,
> We common people nod our heads and loudly cry,
> "How true!"

Life is half spent before we know what it is.

Though the most must be players, some must be spectators.

Is it intelligence that enables a man to get along without education, or is it education which enables the man to get along without the use of his intelligence?

Towering is the confidence of twenty-one!

Nothing is little that feels it with great sensibility.

Every man's affairs, however little, are important to himself.

> Vessels large may venture more,
> But little boats should keep near shore.

Little strokes fell great oaks.

It can happen in the best of regulated families.

If necessary, fail not to eat humble pie with an appetite.

He who excuses himself accuses himself.

By a small sample we may judge of the whole piece.

> A string may jar in the best master's hand,
> And the most skillful archer miss his aim.

He bids fair to grow wise who has discovered that he is not wise.

A noble mind disdains not to repent.

Forbear to judge, for we are sinners all.

> Judge not, that ye be not judged. For with what judgment ye judge, ye shall be judged: and with what measure ye mete, it shall be measured to you again.
>
> Matthew 7:1, 2

Do as I say, not as I do.

Win without boasting.

Lose without excuse.

They are proud in humility; proud in that they are not proud.

It is better to know nothing than to know what ain't so.

Knowledge is of two kinds: we know a subject ourselves, or we know where we can find information on it.

How little I have gained,
How vast the unattained!

Knowledge is proud that he has learned so much;
Wisdom is humble that he knows no more.

And don't confound the language of the nation
With long-tailed words in osity and ation.

Nothing in education is so astonishing as the amount of ignorance it accumulates in inert facts.

A little learning is a dangerous thing.

The great ocean of truth lies all undiscovered before me. Occasionally I find a smooth pebble or a prettier shell than ordinary.

> How many a thing which we cast to the ground,
> When others pick it up becomes a gem!

> Mark how his fame rings out from zone to zone.
> A thousand critics shouting, "He's unknown."

Talent is that which is in man's power; genius is that in whose power a man is.

> "A commonplace life," we say, and we sigh;
> But why should we sigh as we say?
> The commonplace sun in the commonplace sky
> Makes up the commonplace day.

Common sense is not so common.

> One taper lights a thousand,
> Yet shines as it has shone;
> And the humblest light may kindle
> A brighter than its own.

The by-product is sometimes more valuable than the product.

Great flame follows a tiny spark.

Even a single hair casts its shadow.

Union gives strength.

I'm not the only pebble on the beach.

Daughter am I in my mother's house;
But mistress in my own.

Your strength can compensate for my weakness.

United we stand, divided we fall.

The pride of ancestry increases in the ratio of distance.

Give plenty of what is given to you,
And listen to pity's call;
Don't think the little you give is great
And the much you get is small.

If we could see ourselves as others see us,
It would from many a blunder and foolish notion
free us.

God knows I am not what I should be
Nor am I even what I could be.

Learn to see in another's calamity the ills which you should avoid.

It is easy to be brave from a safe distance.

My pride fell with my fortunes.

What small potatoes we all are, compared with what we might be!

In the world I fill up a place which may be better supplied when I have made it empty.

All we have is loaned to us by God.

All art is but an imitation of Nature.

A Rose is sweeter in the bud than full blown.

Large streams from little fountains flow,
Tall oaks from little acorns grow.

Beware of all enterprises that require new clothes.

Yes, and no, and maybe so, and maybe not.

Courage, brother! do not stumble,
Though thy path be dark as night;
There's a star to guide the humble,
Trust in God and do the Right.

The wisest of them all professed to know this only, that he nothing knew.

The wise man does not fancy that he is so at all.

In me there dwells
No greatness, save it be some far off touch
Of greatness to know well I am not great.

He has not lived ill who at his birth and at his death has passed unnoticed.

That favorite subject, Myself!

'Tis a little thing
To give a cup of water; yet its draught
Of cool refreshment, drained by fevered lips
May give a shock of pleasure to the frame

More exquisite than when nectarean juice
Renews the life of joy in happiest hours.

> . . . whosoever shall give you a cup of water to drink in my name, because ye belong to Christ, verily I say unto you, he shall not lose his reward.
>
> Mark 9:41

It is true greatness to have in one the frailty of a man and the security of God.

> . . . My grace is sufficient for thee: for my strength is made perfect in weakness . . . .
>
> 2 Corinthians 12:9

But for the grace of God,
Where would I be?
What would I be?

> Wherefore lay apart all filthiness and superfluity of naughtiness, and receive with meekness the engrafted word, which is able to save your souls.
>
> James 1:21

It is said that George Washington Carver first asked the Lord why He made the universe. Then he asked Him why He made man. Finally, he asked Him, why did you make the peanut?

Lord, of the days that are left to me,
I give them to Thy hand;
Take me and break me and mould me
To the pattern Thou hast planned.

Temperance

The web of our life is of a mingled yarn, good and ill together.

Moderation is the silken string running through the pearl chain of all virtues.

No rule is so general but admits some exception.

Be wisely worldly, but not worldly wise.

> Behold, I [Jesus] send you forth as sheep in the midst of wolves: be ye therefore wise as serpents, and harmless as doves.
>
> Matthew 10:16

If all the skies were sunshine,
Our faces would be fain
To feel once more upon them
The cooling splash of rain.

Courage is a virtue only in proportion as it is directed by prudence.

If you can meet with Triumph and Disaster
And treat those two impostors just the same.
If you can talk with crowds and keep your virtue,
Or walk with Kings—nor lose the common touch.
Yours is the Earth and everything that's in it,
And—which is more—you'll be a Man, my son!

Don't just look at the price. Know the value.

Be not too zealous; moderation is best in all things.

Slight not what is near through aiming at what is far.

Have not too many irons in the fire.

O wonderful, wonderful, and most wonderfully wonderful! and yet again wonderful, and after that whoopee!

From the sublime to the ridiculous is but a step.

In all abundance there is lack.

Nothing in excess!

Do you own your estate or does your estate own you?

How many things there are which I do not need!

Too much rest itself becomes a pain.

Why give your sum of more
To those that have too much?

The best of things, beyond their measure, are not enjoyed.

More is not necessarily better.

Give me not meat so dressed and sauced and seasoned that I don't know whether it is beef or mutton, flesh, fowl, or good red herring.

I can recall our passing to my husband's mother steak-sauce and ketchup, urging her to put it on her steak, saying that it would taste better, and she replied, "I don't want it to taste any better."

He has no leisure who uses it not.

I cannot be angry with you for disagreeing with me. In a few days I may have changed my opinion.

Much outcry, little outcome.

Beware lest you lose the substance by grasping at the shadow.

> Praise from a friend, or censure from a foe,
> Are lost on hearers that our merits know.

We must adjust to changing times but hold to principles that are unchanging.

Life being very short, and the quiet hours few, we ought to waste none of them in reading valueless books.

Life is too short for reading inferior books.

All books are in two classes: the books of the hour, and the books of all times.

Whatever you teach, be brief, that your reader's mind can comprehend and faithfully retain your words. Everything superfluous slips from the full heart.

There are few brains that would not be better for living off their own fat a little while.

Listening is the most important part of the art of conversation.

Wise men profit more by fools than fools by wise men.

There's nothing wrong with having nothing to say, just as long as you don't say it out loud.

If you have not slept, or if you have slept, or if you have a headache, or sciatica, or leprosy, or thunder-stroke, hold your peace.

A wise old owl sat on an oak,
The more he saw the less he spoke;
The less he spoke the more he heard;
Why am I not like that wise old bird?

Men govern nothing with more difficulty than their tongues.

The boneless tongue, so small and weak,
Can crush and kill, declares the Greek.

The tongue destroys a greater horde,
The Turk asserts, than does the sword.

It is not every question that deserves an answer.

A Persian proverb wisely saith,
A lengthy tongue—an early death:
Or sometimes takes this form instead,
Don't let your tongue cut off your head.

Conversation is one of the greatest pleasures in life, but it wants leisure.

The tongue can speak a word whose speed,
Say the Chinese, outstrips the steed.

While Arab sages this impart:
The tongue's great storehouse is the heart.

From Hebrew wit the maxim sprung,
Though feet should slip, ne'er let the tongue.

The sacred writer crowns the whole:
Who keeps the tongue doth keep the soul.

It's a very odd thing—
As odd as can be—
That whatever I eat
Turns into me.

Eat not to dullness; drink not to elevation.

Abstinence is as easy for me as temperance would be difficult.

Why talk to the belly? It has no ears.

Rather than live that you may eat and drink, eat and drink that you may live.

Enough is as good as a feast.

'Tis not the drinking that is to be blamed, but the excess.

I see no objection to stoutness, in moderation.

Bad habits gather by unseen degrees,
As brooks make rivers which run to seas.

Refrain now,
And that shall lend a kind of easiness
To the next abstinence; the next more easy;
For use almost can change the stamp of nature.

Take it or leave it.

Moderation is best, and to avoid all extremes.

The rainbow does not need another hue.

To add another hue to the rainbow would be wasteful and ridiculous excess.

> If all the years were playing holidays,
> To sport would be as tedious as to work.

Too much rest is rust.

Do not shorten the morning by getting up late.

Prosperity is not without many fears and distastes; and adversity is not without comforts and hopes.

Paint costs nothing—such are its preserving qualities.

Spare the rod and spoil the child.

When I give you an inch, you want a mile.

Leap not out of the frying pan into the fire.

Forewarned is forearmed.

One sword keeps another in its sheath.

Everybody's business is nobody's business.

To learn to give, one must know how to take.

It seldom happens that any felicity comes so pure as not to be tempered and alloyed by some mixture of sorrow.

If you should lay up even a little upon a little, and do this often, soon would even this become great.

. . . at the bottom, saving comes too late.

If you don't have it, don't spend it.

Whatever you have, spend less.

Some people have yearnings for equal division of unequal earnings.

Draw your salary before spending it.

The more is given, the less the people will work for themselves, and the less they work, the more their poverty will increase.

The real trouble with money is that you can use it only once.

> Agree with thine adversary quickly, whiles thou art in the way with him . . . [else pay] . . . the uttermost farthing.
>
> Matthew 5:25, 26

A little fire may be quickly extinguished.
Leave it alone and rivers cannot quench.

When Fortune smiles, I smile to think
How quickly she will frown.

You will find rest from vain fancies if you do every act in life as though it were your last.

No man ever became extremely wicked all at once.

Whatever is unknown is magnified.

> Oh, many a shaft at random sent
> Finds mark the archer little meant!
> And many a word at random spoken,
> May sooth or wound a heart that's broken!

To have—to hold—and—in time—let go!

I think it must be time to cast away, for I can't remember where I put the things I keep.

Man builds no structure which outlives a book, but a big book is a big nuisance.

> It is not raining rain to me,
> It's raining daffodils;
> In every dimpled drop I see
> Wild flowers on the hills.

Faith

And this be our motto—
"In God is our trust!"

Ay, call it holy ground,
The soil where first they trod!
They have left unstained what there they found—
Freedom to worship God!

God abides and in man's heart
Speaks with the clear unconquerable cry
Of energies and hope that cannot die.

There are no atheists in the foxholes.

> To see a world in a grain of sand
> And a heaven in a wild flower,
> Hold infinity in the palm of your hand
> And eternity in an hour.
>
> He who doubts from what he sees
> Will ne'er believe, do what you please.

And he [Jesus] said unto him, If they hear not Moses and the prophets, neither will they be persuaded, though one rose from the dead.

Luke 16:31

> For want of me the world's course will not fail:
> When all its work is done, the lie shall rot;
> The truth is great, and shall prevail,
> When none cares whether it prevail or not.

God's kingdom will come whether I help or not.

> The Moving Finger writes; and, having writ,
> Moves on: nor all your Piety nor Wit
> Shall lure it back to cancel half a Line,
> Nor all your Tears wash out a Word of it.

Hope against hope, and ask till ye receive.

> Do you know that yesterday, its aim and reason
> Works you well today for worthier things?
> Then calmly wait the morrow's hidden season,
> And fear you not whatever it brings.

. . . men ought always to pray, and not to faint.
Luke 18:1

Ask, and it shall be given you; seek, and ye shall find; knock, and it shall be opened unto you: For every one that asketh receiveth; and he that seeketh findeth; and to him that knocketh it shall be opened.
Matthew 7:7, 8

We feel that we are greater than we know.

There are two carefree days on which I do not worry: Yesterday and Tomorrow.

The untutored mind can see God in clouds, or hear Him in the wind.

Hope in the soul
Sings the tune without the words,
And never stops at all.

You can't change the past, but you can ruin the good present by worrying about the future.

I am going to seek a great perhaps.

All things are in the hands of God!

With doubt and dismay you are smitten,
You think there's no chance for you, son?
Why, the best books haven't been written
[barring the Bible]
The best race hasn't been won.

To trust God completely is true love.

Trust God to weave your thread into the great web though the pattern shows it not yet.

Why should a man certain of immortality think of his life at all?

> Only through God can come the great awakening;
> Wrong cannot right the wrongs that Wrong has done;
> Only through God, all other gods forsaking,
> Can we attain the heights that must be won.

I have put all my eggs in one basket and then I gave the basket to God.

> Some of your hurts you have cured,
> And the sharpest you still have survived,
> But what torments of grief you endure
> From evils which never arrived!

The prayers most granted are those which seem most denied.

> Let tomorrow take care of tomorrow,
> Leave things of the future to fate;
> What's the use to anticipate sorrow?
> Life's troubles never come too late.

> Surely goodness and mercy shall follow me all the days of my life: and I will dwell in the house of the Lord for ever.
> Psalms 23:6

> What we anticipate seldom occurs;
> What we least expected generally happens.

My degree of acceptance is my only limitation.

God is on time in every promise and prophesy.

God has His ways of leading us and guiding us in ways that we know not.

Prayer is commitment to God. We will do our best to make our prayers come true.

I kneel in my closet and I invite God and His angels in, and when they are there, I neglect God and His angels for the noise of a fly, the sound of a motor or the whining of a door.

Almost every one when age,
Disease, or sorrows strike him,
Inclines to think there is a God,
Or something very like Him.

I tremble for myself, my family, my country, and the world when I reflect that God is just.

I take comfort when I recall His mercy endures for ever!

Prayer is the soul's greatest privilege, its hardest labor, its purest joy.

Upon God's will I lay me down,
As child upon its mother's breast;
No silken couch, nor softest bed,
Could ever give me such sweet rest.

> Have mercy upon me, O God, according to thy lovingkindness: according unto the multitude of thy tender mercies blot out my transgressions. Wash me throughly from mine iniquity, and cleanse me from my sin . . . wash me, and I shall be whiter than snow.
>
> Psalms 51:1, 2, 7

Every wish is like a prayer with God.

More things are wrought by prayer
Than this world dreams of. Wherefore, let
thy voice
Rise like a fountain for me night and day.

I believe all Christians agree in the essentials and that their differences are trivial.

Brother, the creed would stifle me
That shelters you.

Find me men on earth today
Who care enough to pray!

'Tis God alone Who rules the world,
Enthroned above the skies;
Who brings a nation to decay
Or bids a nation rise.

Blessed is the nation whose God is the Lord . . . .
Psalms 33:12

For truth is precious and divine,
Too rich a pearl for carnal swine.

Give not that which is holy unto the dogs, neither cast ye your pearls before swine, lest they trample them under their feet, and turn again and rend you.

Matthew 7:6

I do not question school nor creed
Of Christian, Protestant, or Priest;
I only know that creeds to me
Are but new names for mystery,
That good is good from west to east,
And more I do not know nor need
To know, to love my neighbor well.

There is nothing so powerful as truth.

Leave the matter of religion to the family altar, the Church, and the private school, supported entirely by contributions. Keep the Church and the State for ever separate.

Do not swallow more belief than you can digest.

Truth never yet fell dead in the streets; it has such affinity with the world of men, the seed however broadcast will catch somewhere and produce its hundredfold.

Truth is one forever absolute.

. . . thy word is truth.
John 17:17

If I believe not God's words, I either have a false interpretation of Scripture or a misconception of Science.

And better had they ne'er been born
Who read the Bible to doubt or to scorn.

. . . be ready always to give an answer to every man that asketh you a reason of the hope that is in you with meekness and fear.

1 Peter 3:15

Strong Son of God, immortal Love,
Whom we, that have not seen Thy face,
By faith, and faith alone, embrace
Believing where we cannot prove.

It could best be felt when it could not be clearly seen.

And so, I thought, the anvil of God's Word
For ages skeptic blows have beat upon;
Yet though the noise of falling blows was heard
The anvil is unharmed—the hammers gone.

Truth is on the march and nothing can stop it.

Through faith we understand that the worlds were framed by the word of God, so that things which are seen were not made of things which do appear.

Hebrews 11:3

The man who knows and knows he knows is a man of faith.

. . . faith cometh by hearing, and hearing by the word of God.

Romans 10:17

[Jesus said:] If ye continue in my word, then are ye my disciples indeed; And ye shall know the truth, and the truth shall make you free.

John 8:31, 32

Verily, verily, I say unto you, He that heareth my word, and believeth on him that sent me, hath everlasting life, and shall not come into condemnation; but is passed from death unto life.

John 5:24

Christ is a path, if any be misled;
He is a robe, if any naked be;
If any chance to hunger, He is bread;
If any be a bondman, He is free;
If any be but weak, how strong is He!

. . . we look not at the things which are seen, but at the things which are not seen: for the things which are seen are temporal; but the things which are not seen are eternal.

2 Corinthians 4:18

Every good gift and every perfect gift is from above, and cometh down from the Father of lights, with whom is no variableness, neither shadow of turning.

James 1:17

The Lord who made your teeth will give you bread.

There is no gain except by loss;
There is no life except by death;
There is no vision but by faith.

Refresh your inner life daily by reading a portion of the Bible.

There's a time for some things,
and a time for all things;
a time for great things,
and a time for small things.

The Christian life is an obtainment rather than an attainment.

Our vows are heard betimes! and Heaven takes care
To grant, before we can conclude the prayer:
Preventing angels met it half the way,
And sent us back to praise, who came to pray.

Sometime the "why" is plain as the way to parish Church.

When I thought to know this, it was too painful for me;
Until I went into the sanctuary of God; then understood
I . . . .

Psalms 73:16, 17

All the world's a stage,
And all the men and women merely players.
They have their exits and their entrances;
And one man in his time plays many parts.

Some keep the Sabbath going to Church,
Others keep it staying at home,
With a bobolink for a chorister,
And an orchard for a dome.

All the while my Lord I meet
In every land, in every street.

If I were damned of body and soul,
I know whose prayers would make me whole,
Mother o' mine, O Mother o' mine.

And if a lowly singer dries one tear,
Or soothes one humble human heart in pain,
Be sure his homely verse to God is dear,
And not one stanza has been sung in vain.

The worldly Hope men set their hearts upon
Turns to ashes or it prospers; and anon,
Like snow upon the Desert's dusty face,
Lighting a little hour or two—is gone.

I can see God everywhere and in everyone!

Talk Faith. The world is better off without
Your uttered ignorance and morbid doubt.

Every cloud engenders not a storm.

No one knows what he can do till he tries.

You should hammer your iron while it is glowing hot.

You may have inherited your aptitude, but your determination is your own.

Throw not sand against the wind, for the wind will blow it back again.

Hope is the belief that joy will come; desire is the wish it may come.

Take short views, hope for the best, and trust in God.

No seed shall perish which the soul hath sown.

> Pray for peace and grace and spiritual food,
> For wisdom and guidance, for all these are good,
> But don't forget the potatoes.

Bait the hook well; the fish will bite.

> The surest plan to make a man
> Is think him so.

He who mistrusts most should be trusted the least.

Do not count your chickens before they are hatched.

Refrain from peering too far.

> In idle wishes fools supinely stay;
> Be there a will, and wisdom finds a way.

> Nothing that is can pause or stay;
> The moon will wax, the moon will wane,
> The mist and cloud will turn to rain,
> The rain to mist and cloud again,
> Tomorrow be today.

No counsel is more trustworthy than that which is given upon ships that are in peril.

> . . . in him [the Lord] we live, and move, and have our being . . . .
>
> Acts 17:28

Everything I do is a miracle!

All things come of Thee, have their being in Thee, and return to Thee.

I am a miracle!

To me every hour of the light and dark is a miracle!
Every cubic inch of space is a miracle!

The Almighty has His Own purposes.

God and all the attributes of God are eternal.

And One born in a manger
Rules the world!

> . . . All power is given unto me [Jesus] in heaven and in earth.
>
> Matthew 28:18

> Except the Lord build the house, they labour in vain that build it: except the Lord keep the city, the watchman waketh but in vain.
>
> Psalms 127:1

> The horse is prepared against the day of battle: but safety is of the Lord.
>
> Proverbs 21:31

A liar will not be believed, even when he speaks the truth.

The boy called out, "Wolf, Wolf!" and the villagers came out to help him. "I was only funnin'." A few days afterward he tried the same trick, and again they came to his help. Shortly after this a wolf actually came, but this time the villagers thought the boy was deceiving them again, and nobody came to his call.

It is not the oath that makes us believe the man, but the man the oath.

God sends the sun, He sends the shower,
Alike they are needful to the flower;
And joys and tears alike are sent
To give the soul fit nourishment.
As comes to me, or cloud or sun,
Father, Thy will, not mine, be done!

How oft the darkest hour of ill
Breaks brightest into dawn.

It is a long road that knows no turning.

My soul fainteth for thy salvation: but I hope in thy word.
Psalms 119:81

I need not shout my faith, Thrice eloquent
Are quiet trees and the green listening sod—
Hushed are the stars, whose power is never spent;
The hills are mute—yet how they speak of God!

Just as there are songs without words, there are prayers without words.

Never yet was a springtime,
Late though lingered the snow,
That the sap stirred not at the whisper
Of the southwind, sweet and low;
Never yet was a springtime
When the buds forgot to blow.

While the earth remaineth, seedtime and harvest, and cold and heat, and summer and winter, and day and night shall not cease.

Genesis 8:22

Is not God upon the ocean and in the air above
Just the same as on the land?

What God ordains is always good:
No wrong His will intends.
In wisdom He directs my course
And all my trouble ends.
Why should I fear when He is near?
Tho' need and want o'ertake me,
He will never forsake me!

What God ordains is always good:
And though the cup selected
Too bitter to my taste may seem,
It must not be rejected.
For in the end God help will send;
He will dispel all sadness
And fill my soul with gladness.

What God ordains is always good:
Here shall my stand be taken;
Tho' dark and lone my way appear,
I shall not be forsaken.
In God's embrace I have a place;
His loving arms will shield me,
And so to Him I yield me.

I thank Thee, Saviour, for the grief
Thy goodness bids me bear,
And for each word of sweet relief,
That saves me from despair.

I see but dimly all Thy ways,
Nor may each purpose tell,
But this I know to wake my praise:
Thou doest all things well.

How lovely are the faces of
Those who talk with God . . .
Lit with an inner sureness of
The path their feet have trod;
How gentle is the manner of
Those who walk with Him!
No strength can overcome them, and
No cloud their courage dim.
Keen are the hands and feet—ah, yes,
Of those who wait His will,
And clear as crystal mirrors are
The hearts His love can fill.

I have a life in Christ to live,
I have a death in Christ to die;
And must I wait till Science give
All doubts a full reply?
Nay, rather while the sea of doubt
Is raging wildly round about,
Questioning of Life and Death and Sin,
Let me but creep within
Thy fold, O Christ! and at Thy feet
Take but the lowest seat;
And hear Thine awful Voice repeat
In gentle accent, heavenly sweet,
"Come unto Me and rest;
Believe Me and be blest."

I know not what the future holds,
Of good or ill for me and mine;
I only know that God enfolds
Me in His loving arms divine.

So I shall walk the earth in trust
That He who notes the sparrow's fall
Will help me bear whate'er I must
And lend an ear whene'er I call.

It matters not if dreams dissolve
Like mist beneath the morning sun,
For swiftly as the world revolves
So swiftly will life's race be run.

It matters not if hopes depart,
Or life be pressed with toil and care;
If love divine shall fill my heart
And all be sanctified with prayer.

With aching heart within my breast
And body robbed of all its zest,
I find no answer to my quest
And yet, I bless Your Name.

No way to cool this fevered brain,
No drug to soothe this raging pain,
Of doubts and fears I cry in vain
And yet, I bless Your Name.

No longer shall I know the way
Of happiness in yesterday,
These fears I cannot keep at bay
And yet, I bless Your Name.

So often have I cursed Your plan,
That baffles the mere mind of man.
My words the fires of Hell would fan,
And yet, I bless Your Name.

My cross I can no longer bear.
I leave my troubles in Your care,
With grateful and with humble air
For still, I bless Your Name.

O Lord, if only my will may remain right and firm towards Thee, do with me whatsoever it shall please Thee. For it cannot be anything but good, whatsoever Thou shalt do with me.

If it be Thy will I should be in darkness, be Thou blessed; and, if it be Thy will I should be in light, be Thou again blessed, and if Thou wilt have me afflicted, be Thou equally blessed. If Thou vouchsafe to comfort me, be Thou blessed; O Lord! for Thy sake I will cheerfully suffer whatever shall come on me with Thy permission.

Then let me learn submission sweet
In every thought, in each desire,
And humbly lay at His dear feet
A heart aglow with heavenly fire.

Ideals are like stars; you will not succeed in touching them with your hands. But like the seafaring man, on the desert of waters, you choose them as your guide, and following them you will reach your destiny!

Be not afraid of life.
Believe that life is worth living and your belief
will help create the fact.

Life Eternal

My heart is sore pained within me: and the terrors of death are fallen upon me. Fearfulness and trembling are come upon me, and horror hath overwhelmed me. And I said, Oh that I had wings like a dove! for then would I fly away, and be at rest.

Psalms 55:4–6

What age, ache, penury and imprisonment
Can lay on nature, is a paradise
To what we fear of death.

Everybody wants to go to heaven, but few want to die to get there.

Fear not the sentence of death. Remember them that have been before you and that come after; for this is the sentence of the Lord over all flesh. And why are you against the pleasure of the most High?

No one has reached maturity until he has learned to face the fact of his own death and shaped his way of living accordingly.

If you are willing to take the Bible as authority, I believe your fear of death can be dispelled, because by faith we see beyond the grave.

It is well that we

Reflect upon our mortal state,
How frail our life, how short the date;
There is no one that draws breath
Safe from disease, secure from death.

It lies around us like a cloud,
A world we do not see;
Yet the closing of an eye
May bring us there to be.

O why should the spirit of mortal be proud?
Like a fast-flitting meteor, a fast-flying cloud,
A flash of the lightning, a break of the wave,
He passes from life to his rest in the grave.

'Tis the wink of an eye, 'tis the draught of a breath,
From the blossom of health to the paleness of death.

As he came forth of his mother's womb, naked shall he return to go as he came, and shall take nothing of his labour, which he may carry away in his hand.

Ecclesiastes 5:15

Yes, Death is at the bottom of the cup,
And every one that lives must drink it up;
And yet between the sparkle at the top
And the black lees where lurks that bitter drop,
There swims enough good liquor, Heaven knows,
To ease our hearts of all their other woes.

Death argues not displeasure. It was not Adam or Cain who died first, but Abel, the innocent and righteous.

Strange, is it not? that of the myriads who before us
passed the door of Darkness through,
Not one returns to tell us of the Road, which to discover,
we must travel, too.

Ah Christ, that it were possible
For one short hour to see
The souls we loved, that they might tell us
What and where they be.

Although we believe we shall inherit eternal bliss when we die, we do not wish to talk of such unpleasant subjects.

Death breaks all chains and sets all captives free.

Death breaks every bond. The whole world has no power over the dead.

As men, we are all equal in the presence of death.

Death, with impartial step, knocks at the poor man's cottage and at the palace of the King.

> The tall, the wise, the reverent head
> Must lie as low as ours.

> To Death we must stoop, be we high, be we low,
> But how and how suddenly, few be that know.

> All human beings are subject to decay,
> And, when God summons, all must obey.

Death levels all ranks and lays the shepherd's crook beside the scepter.

> When Life knocks at the door no one can wait,
> When Death makes his arrest, we have to go.

We get into such a habit of living that we do not wish to die.

Death in itself is nothing; but the fear to be we know not what, we know not where.

The sense of death is most in apprehension.

The fear of death is more to be dreaded than death itself.

Our death is one thing that is truly our own.

Death we call it, but there is no death!

God never wasted a leaf on a tree. He will not squander a soul.

Eternal life is harmony with the true order of things—life in God.

Death cannot kill what never dies.

We cannot go where God is not.

> For God so loved the world, that he gave his only begotten Son, that whosoever believeth in him should not perish, but have everlasting life.
>
> John 3:16

Yes, none other Name is given
Unto any under heaven
Whereby souls in mortal strife
Rise to gain eternal life.

And this is the comfort of the good,
That the grave cannot hold them
And that they live as soon as they die.
For Death is no more than a turning of
 us over from time to eternity.

To think of Death should not make us sad but more watchful, industrious, cheerful and thankful to God for taking away the sting of death through faith in Jesus Christ.

See how we trifle here below,
Fond of these earthly toys;
Our souls, how heavily they go
To reach eternal joys.

A good life, a clean conscience, an honest heart, and well-ordered conversation is the only remedy I know for fearing Death.

Death is the golden key that opens the palace of eternity.

I am that blessing which men fly from—Death.

The night with its terrors, its darkness, its feverish dreams is passing away; and when we awake it will be into the sunlight of God.

Fear not, Jesus is with us; He will never leave us nor forsake us.

> Christ leads us through no darker rooms
> Than He went through before;
> Whoever to God's kingdom comes,
> Must enter by this door.

Thanks to Jesus Who has promised to conduct the faithful through Death to everlasting delight.

> . . . Master, What shall I do to inherit eternal life? And he answering said, Thou shalt love the Lord thy God with all thy heart, and with all thy soul, and with all thy strength, and with all thy mind; and thy neighbour as thyself . . . this do, and thou shalt live.
>
> Luke 10:25, 27, 28

My sheep hear my voice, and I know them, and they follow me: And I give unto them eternal life; and they shall never perish, neither shall any man pluck them out of my hand.

John 10:27, 28

Jesus gave His life for me
That I might have life eternally!

Jesus came that we might have life and have it more abundantly. If we learn how to live, we shall have learned how to die.

Jesus by His death took away the bitterness and sting of death.

Walk in the light! and even the tomb
No fearful shade shall wear;
Faith shall chase away its gloom,
For Christ has conquered there.

In the way of righteousness is life; and in the pathway thereof there is no death.

Proverbs 12:28

Then shall the dust return to the earth as it was: and the spirit shall return unto God who gave it.

Ecclesiastes 12:7

Live well; how long or how short leave to God.

. . . Let me die the death of the righteous, and let my last end be like his!

Numbers 23:10

Who, that has ever been,
Could bear to be no more?
Yet who would tread again the scene
He trod through life before?
[But if I had to do it all over again, my dear husband, I would rather do it with you.]

As life runs on, the road grows strange
With faces new, and near the end
The milestones into headstones change,
'Neath every one a friend.

Pity for the living—
Envy for the dead.

So God deals with us and takes away
Our playthings one by one, and by the hand
Leads us to rest.

As long as there is death, there is hope.

We shall some day leave off the clay
And rise to higher planes of life.

There is no death! What seems so is transition.

There is no such thing as death in the sense that life has ceased.

Life is a predicament which precedes death.

It is as natural to man to die as to be born.

God conceals from men the happiness of death that they may endure life.

Death is not the end of life, but an event in life.

> Verily, verily, I say unto you, If a man keep my saying, he shall never see death.
>
> John 8:51

> And this is the promise that He hath promised us, even eternal life.
>
> 1 John 2:25

> . . . because I live, ye shall live also.
>
> John 14:19

Death cannot separate us from the love of God which is in Christ Jesus our Lord.

Life eternal is to know that God is love, and that nothing can separate those who love. In recognizing this truth, death loses its reality.

God has made for man an earthly habitation,
The body soil in which the soul may grow.
This little life is but the preparation—
My soul does know.

Do not let your heart be troubled,
Neither let it be afraid,
Lean upon the precious promise
That the blessed Master made.

Keep yourselves in the love of God, looking for the mercy of our Lord Jesus Christ unto eternal life.

Life is the childhood of our immortality.

A man is not completely born until he is dead. Why, then, should we grieve that a new child is born among the immortals.

If our sight could clearly distinguish the opposite bank, who would remain at the tempestuous coast of time?

> Proclaim to every people, tongue and nation
> That God in Whom they live and move, is Love:
> Tell how He stooped to save His lost creation
> And died on earth that man might live above.

> And he [the thief on the cross] said unto Jesus, Lord, remember me when thou comest into thy kingdom. And Jesus said unto him, Verily I say unto thee, To day shalt thou be with me in paradise.
>
> Luke 23:42, 43

> Thou, Who in a manger
> Once has lowly lain,
> You do now in glory
> O'er all kingdoms reign.

> Good Christian men, rejoice,
> With heart, and soul, and voice;
> Now you need not fear the grave;
> Jesus Christ was born to save.

Awake, my soul and sing
Of Christ Who died for me,
Who died eternal life to bring
And lives that death may die!

No eye has seen, no ear has heard,
Nor sense, nor reason known,
What joys the Father has prepared
For those who love the Son.

. . . Eye hath not seen, nor ear heard, neither have entered into the heart of man, the things which God hath prepared for them that love him.

1 Corinthians 2:9

Glories upon glories has our God prepared,
For the souls that love Him, one day to be shared;
Eye has not beheld them, Ear has never heard;
Nor of these has uttered thought or speech a word.

And as we have borne the image of the earthy, we shall also bear the image of the heavenly.

1 Corinthians 15:49

O how glorious and resplendent,
Fragile body, shall you be,
When endued with heavenly beauty,
Full of health, and strong, and free;
Full of vigor, full of pleasure,
That shall last eternally!

Dear Lord, help us prepare
For that eventful day

When our undying souls shall leave
This tenement of clay.

To us, O Lord, the wisdom give
Each passing moment so to spend,
That we at length with Thee may live
Where life and bliss shall never end.

That delightful day will come
When my dear Lord will bring me home,
And I shall see His Face!

Soon shall my eyes behold Thee,
With rapture, face to face;
One half has not been told me
Of all Thy power and grace;
Thy beauty, Lord, and glory,
The wonders of Thy love
Shall be the endless story
Of all the saints above.

As for me, I will behold thy face in righteousness: I shall be satisfied, when I awake with thy likeness.

Psalms 17:15

Verily, verily, I say unto you, He that heareth my word, and believeth on him that sent me, hath everlasting life, and shall not come into condemnation; but is passed from death unto life.

John 5:24

Death is the most dramatic of all the phenomena of life.

The belief that we shall never die is the foundation of living and dying well.

> On death and judgment, heaven and hell
> Who oft does think, must needs die well.

Be prepared for death and death or life will be sweeter.

We begin to understand Death when one of our own loved ones dies.

Each departed one is like a magnet that attracts us to the next world.

> There is no flock, however watched and tended,
> But one dead lamb is there!
> There is no fireside, howsoever defended,
> But has one vacant chair!

> When, musing on companions gone,
> We doubly feel ourselves alone,
> And the tear we shed, though in secret it rolls,
> Shall long keep his memòry green in our souls.

> Grief fills the room up of my absent child,
> Lies in his bed, walks up and down with me,
> Puts on his pretty looks, repeats his words,
> Reminds me of all his gracious parts,
> Stuffs out his vacant garments with his form.

We do not want to lose our grief because our grief is bound up with our love and we could not cease to mourn without being robbed of our affection.

Silence is no certain token
That no secret grief is there;
Sorrow which is never spoken
Is the heaviest load to bear.

Give sorrow words; the grief
that does not speak
Whispers the o'er fraught heart
and bids it break.

To weep is to make less the depth of grief.

While grief is fresh, every attempt to divert only irritates.

Never does one feel so utterly helpless as in trying to speak comfort for great bereavement.

Christ's Easter puts Death in its proper perspective. His Resurrection denies that Death is the end of life. He has proven that Death is the beginning of life and the key to the meaning of life.

God will not take the spirits which He gave, and make the glorified so new that they are lost to you and me.

When Death strikes down the innocent and young, for every fragile form from which he lets the panting spirit free, a hundred virtues rise, in shapes of mercy, charity, and love, to walk the world and bless it.

She sparkled, exhaled, and went to heaven.

Our very hopes belied our fears,
Our fears our hopes belied;
We thought her dying when she slept,
And sleeping when she died.

When she had passed, it seemed like the ceasing of exquisite music.

God's finger touched him, and he slept.

God saw the road was getting steep,
The hill too hard to climb
So he gently closed his loving eyes to sleep
And whispered, "Peace, Be Ever Thine."

He lives, he wakes—'tis Death is dead, not he.

O fuller, sweeter is that life,
And larger, ampler is the air:
Eye cannot see nor heart conceive
The glory there;

Nor yet know to what high purpose Thou
Dost yet employ their ripened powers,
Nor how at Thy behest they touch
This life of ours.

It is better to go to the house of mourning, than to go to the house of feasting . . . the living will lay it to his heart. Sorrow is better than laughter: for by the sadness of the countenance the heart is made better.

Ecclesiastes 7:2, 3

O yes, it's hard
To understand
Why some must go so young,
Before they've time
To dream their dreams,
Before their songs are sung.
Could there be greater
Work for them,
Or possible release
From something where
They cannot find
An answer to their peace?
It must be that our lives
Are planned,
"We have a time to go"—
May faith help us
To understand
What we can't see or know.

Three years she grew in sun and shower,
Then God said, "A lovelier flower
On earth was never sown;
This child I to Myself will take;
She shall be Mine, and I will make
a Lady of My Own."

Sleep on, beloved, sleep and take thy rest
Lay down thy head upon thy Saviour's breast.
We love thee well, but Jesus loves thee best.
—Good-night.

That divinest hope, which none can know of
Who have not laid their dearest in the grave.

He that lacks time to mourn lacks time to mend.
Eternity mourns that.

The grave itself is but a covered bridge leading from light to light, through a brief darkness.

Lord, it belongs not to our care
Whether we die or live;
To love and serve Thee be our share,
For this Thy grace must give.

To neglect, at any time, preparation for death, is to sleep on our post at a siege; to omit it in old age, is to sleep at an attack.

I know death has ten thousand several doors for men to take their exit.

The martyr first, whose eagle eye
Could pierce beyond the grave,
Who saw his Master in the sky
And called on Him to save;
Like Him, with pardon on his tongue,
In midst of mortal pain,
He prayed for them that did the wrong.
Who follows in his train?

And they stoned Stephen, calling upon God, and saying, Lord Jesus receive my spirit. And he kneeled down, and cried with a loud voice, Lord, lay not this sin to their charge. And when he had said this, he fell asleep.
Acts 7:59, 60

Let saints on earth in concert sing
With those whose work is done;
For all the servants of our King
In heaven and earth are one.

One family we dwell in Him,
One Church, above, beneath,
Though now divided by the stream,
The narrow stream of Death.

One army of the living God,
To His command we bow;
Part of the Host have crossed the flood,
And part are crossing now.

Death is only a beautiful adventure.

E'en now by faith we join our hands
With those that went before
And greet the ever-living bands
On the eternal shore.

Jesus, be Thou our constant Guide;
Then, when the word is given,
Bid Jordan's narrow stream divide,
And bring us safe to heaven.

Nor time, nor space, nor deep, nor high,
Can keep my own away from me.

There are no dead; we fall asleep
To awaken where they never weep;
We close our eyes on pain and sin,
Our breath flows out, but life flows in.

Our Father's house is mansioned fair,
Beyond our vision dim;
All souls are His, and here or there
Are living unto Him.

God shall wipe away all tears;
There's no death, no pain, nor fears;
And they count not time by years,
For there is no night there.

O could we make our doubts remove,
Those gloomy doubts that rise,
And view the Canaan that we love,
With beclouded eyes:

Could we but climb where Moses stood
And view the landscape o'er,
Not Jordan's stream, nor death's cold flood,
Could fright us from the shore.

We know in part: enough we know
To walk with God, and walk aright;
And He shall guide us as we go,
And lead us into fuller light,
Till, when we stand before His throne,
We know at last as we are known.

For now we see through a glass, darkly; but then face to face: now I know in part: but then shall I know even as also I am known.

1 Corinthians 13:12

Fight on, my soul, till Death
Shall bring me to my God;

He'll take me at my parting breath
To His divine abode.

For this God is our God for ever and ever: he will be our guide even unto death.

Psalms 48:14

As we enter into death's shade,
Our Saviour's Voice will cheer us:
It is I, be not afraid!

Who knows how soon my days are ended?
My days are few and time speeds on.
How swiftly, in this world of changes,
May death approach and life be gone.

Help me to put my house in order
That I may ever ready be
To leave this world and say in meekness:
Lord, as Thou wilt, deal Thou with me.

O Father, let my sins be covered
With Jesus' blood and righteousness
By faith this spotless garment wearing,
I find relief from all distress.

Prayer is the Christian's vital breath,
The Christian's native air;
His watch-word at the gate of death;
He enters heaven with prayer.

Why should I be afraid to tread the path to my future home?

I have loved life, and I know I shall love death as well.

If such the sweetness of the stream,
What must the fountain be,
Where saints and angels draw their bliss,
O Lord, direct from Thee.

We are traveling home to God,
In the way our fathers trod:
They are happy now, and we
Soon their happiness shall see.

Death is the veil which those who live call life.
They sleep, and it is lifted.

Think of those who have passed away as not held by Death, but held by Love.

Our life is closed, our life begins,
The long, long anchorage we leave,
The ship is clear at last, she leaps!
She swiftly courses from the shore.
Joy, shipmates, Joy!

Give me work, dear Lord, until my life shall end and life till my work is done.

Let me die, working—
Still tackling plans unfinished, tasks undone;
Clean to its end, swift may my race be run.
No laggard steps, no faltering, no shirking:
Let me die, working!

Let me die, thinking—
Let me fare forth still with an open mind,
Fresh secrets to unfold, new truths to find,
My soul undimmed, alert, no question blinking;
Let me die, thinking!

Let me die, laughing—
No sighing o'er past sins; they are forgiven.
Spilled on this earth are all the joys of heaven;
The wine of life, the cup of mirth quaffing:
Let me die, laughing!

I will be as a bridegroom in my death, and run into it as to a lover's bed.

When we've been there ten thousand years,
Bright, shining as the sun,
We've no less days to sing God's praise
Than when we first begun.

Our Father,

Cleanse our eyes, that we may see more clearly. Draw us closer to Thyself, that we may know ourselves nearer to our beloved who are with Thee. And while Thou dost prepare a place for us, prepare us for that happy place, that where they are, and Thou art, We, too may be.

Amen.

Now unto him that is able to keep you from falling, and to present you faultless before the presence of his glory with exceeding joy, To the only wise God our Saviour, be glory and majesty, dominion and power, both now and ever. Amen.

Jude 24, 25